IS THE
NEW TESTAMENT
RELIABLE?

PAUL BARNETT

IVP Academic

An imprint of InterVarsity Press
Downers Grove, Illinois

InterVarsity Press
P.O. Box 1400, Downers Grove, IL 60515-1426
Internet: www.ivpress.com
E-mail: email@ivpress.com

InterVarsity Press® is the book-publishing division of InterVarsity Christian Fellowship/USA®, a student movement active on campus at hundreds of universities, colleges and schools of nursing in the United States of America, and a member movement of the International Fellowship of Evangelical Students. For information about local and regional activities, write Public Relations Dept., InterVarsity Christian Fellowship/USA, 6400 Schroeder Rd., P.O. Box 7895, Madison, WI 53707-7895, or visit the IVCF website at <www.intervarsity.org>.

The Scripture quotations quoted herein are from the Revised Standard Version of the Bible, *copyright 1946, 1952, 1971 by the Division of Christian Education of the National Council of the Churches of Christ in the U.S.A. Used by permission. All rights reserved.*

Chapter twelve originally appeared in The Truth About Jesus *(Sydney: Aquila, 1994).*

Cover design: Cindy Kiple

Cover image: Scala/Art Resource

ISBN 978-0-8308-2768-8

Printed in the United States of America ∞

Library of Congress Cataloging-in-Publication Data

A catalog record for this book is available from the Library of Congress.

P	20	19	18	17	16	15	14	13	12	11	10	9	8
Y	23	22	21	20	19	18	17	16					

CONTENTS

Foreword 9

1   INTRODUCTION: *Is There History?* 11

2   THE QUESTION OF TRUTH 16

3   DID JESUS EXIST? *Early Non-Christian References* 22

4   FIXING THE TIME FRAME 35

5   IS THE TRANSMISSION TRUSTWORTHY? 43

6   THE TWO WITNESSES 48

7   WITNESS ONE: *The Disciple Whom Jesus Loved* 54

8   WITNESS TWO: *Peter Through Mark* 74

9   LUKE AND MATTHEW 89

10 THE BIRTH OF JESUS 98

11 MIRACLES AND THE MODERN WORLD 105

12 THE RESURRECTION OF JESUS 111

13 PAUL AND THE HISTORICAL JESUS 136

14 THE ACTS OF THE APOSTLES 145

15 ARCHAEOLOGY AND THE NEW TESTAMENT:
   "Hard Copy" from Antiquity 159

16 IS THE NEW TESTAMENT
   HISTORICALLY RELIABLE? 165

17 WHO IS JESUS? 176

18 HISTORICAL ORIGINS OF
   CHRISTIANITY AND ISLAM 181

Notes 191

Index 196

FOREWORD

Today, myriad voices claim to tell us the truth in the spiritual realm. So many, in fact, that the search for truth can be confusing. Some may even be tempted to give up the search.

Christianity stands alone in that its claim to reveal the truth relies not on private mystical revelations to a prophet or teacher (revelations that, because of their private nature, cannot be verified or falsified), but on public events, which happened just thirty lifetimes ago in the Middle East.

The New Testament writers assert that at a time and place (we can know where and when), God became man. He was born, grew up, taught with great authority, was crucified and rose again from the dead, and promised that he would bring the judgment day. That these events happened is a matter of public record. They were subject to eyewitnesses, as are other historical events. The uniqueness of this claim to truth lies in the fact that it can be subjected to the laws of evidence, that is, verified or falsified. There is evidence for us to make a decision.

There is no more important question than "Is the New Testament reliable?" The attractiveness of Dr. Paul Barnett's book lies in the clarity and simplicity with which he presents the issues. Dr. Barnett brings great understanding of the ancient world and its non-Christian historians, together with an understanding of the New Testament and its claims to history. He is able to show us external evidence for the historicity of the New Testament, and how this dovetails with the internal evidence. This revised version includes timely new chapters on the resurrection of Jesus and the historical origins of Christianity and Islam.

Dr. Barnett has done us a great favor by demonstrating that there is clear and compelling evidence regarding the historicity of Jesus. He shows us that we really do have an accurate record of the words, actions and significance of Jesus, the focal point of history.

Dr. Peter F. Jensen
Anglican Archbishop of Sydney

1

INTRODUCTION

Is There History?

According to Leopold von Ranke, the father of modern history writers, the aim of the historian is to determine "what actually happened." How feasible is that aim in regard to the New Testament events of two thousand years ago?

Followers of postmodern philosophy argue that von Ranke's aim is unattainable at any time, modern or ancient. They argue that there is no objective entity called "history" but only the "eyes" of individuals who left behind their *impressions* of what happened in the surviving sources. The reality of overpowering subjectivity in witnesses past and present makes the concept of history impossible and the history-writing enterprise problematic.

Postmodernists may be right in their observation that there is no one fixed, objective reality called history. Yet they overstate the case if they say that people and events from the past are inaccessible to present inquiry, blocked by the blinded subjectivity of the human sources of that information.

SUBJECTIVITY IN ANCIENT SOURCES

Scholars of ancient history have always recognized the subjectivity factor in their available sources. It might be observed in passing, with a touch of humor, that they have so few sources available compared to their modern counterparts that they will gladly seize whatever scraps of information that are at hand. Indeed, a major difference between the two disciplines regarding availability of sources is that modern historians have feast, and ancient historians famine.

Ancient historians are familiar with subjectivity in their sources, including biased motivation in writing. Josephus regards Jewish rebels against Roman rule as responsible for the destruction of Jerusalem, so his accounts in his *Jewish War* are written from that perspective. A modern historian's account of a military campaign is likely to be more objective, for example, Antony Beevor's *The Fall of Berlin 1945*, telling the story of the Russian assault on the German capital.[1] True, Beevor writes this history his own way, idiosyncratically, but he does not superimpose upon his account of the fall of Berlin the unrelenting bias we see in Josephus's description of the events leading to the fall of Jerusalem.

Does this render Josephus's account useless? Not at all. When Josephus is describing *events* his account is impressive. We have a cogent, detailed narrative that finds support from archaeology at several points. Rather, it is his spin on the facts that stands out compared to modern writers. It is part of the ancient historian's craft to recognize, account for and accommodate the "special interests" of their sources, whether in a literary text like Josephus's or even in an inscription.

How, then, should we regard the postmodern skepticism about history? It is an exaggerated skepticism. Do we doubt an event like the fall of Jerusalem to the Romans (in A.D. 70) when independent sources (Josephus and Tacitus) describe it? Is there any doubt that Jesus was a genuine figure of history when those who take opposing views about him refer to him (the Gospels and Tacitus)? Independently written accounts of an event are comparable to multiple witnesses of a motor accident; there may be discrepancies in the details, but the basic fact of the event is accepted.

Postmodern insights do have value. In highlighting the power of subjectivity we are reminded of our own potential biases and prejudices. While these are real and can potentially skew our judgment, professional training and criticism by others focus the mind and make significant objectivity attainable. If physicians and accountants are capable of objectivity in their respective disciplines, so too are historians of the past and present. In spite of (extreme) postmodern skepticism, historical research that results in intelligible conclusions is a practical possibility.

LUKE AS A HISTORY WRITER

History writers in antiquity were aware of potential bias and the value of reliable sources and eyewitness evidence. Even today the ideals of the second-century (A.D.) historian Lucian cannot be faulted:

> Facts must not be carelessly put together, but the historian must work with great labour and often at great trouble make inquiry preferably being present and an eyewitness; failing that he must rely on those who are incorruptible, and have no bias from passion, nor add or diminish anything. (*Quomodo* 47)

Lucian called for "great trouble" making "inquiry," relying on sources that are "incorruptible," writing without "bias," neither "adding" nor omitting anything. In the previous century a man named Luke began his seventy-year history of the birth and spread of Christianity in these words:

> Inasmuch as many have undertaken to compile a narrative of the things which have been accomplished among us, just as they were delivered to us by those who from the beginning were eyewitnesses and ministers of the word, it seemed good to me also, having followed all things closely for some time past, to write an orderly account for you, most excellent Theophilus, that you may know the truth concerning the things of which you have been informed. (Lk 1:1-4)

It is as if Luke knew about and was following Lucian's guidelines before they were given! Luke, who declares that he was not an eyewitness, received texts from those who were. He "followed all things closely" and wrote so that his reader, Theophilus, could "know the truth" about the events in the narrative that follow. In other words, Luke wrote according to the best practice of his time.

Luke's was a stunning achievement in those times. His narrative spans the period from the birth of John the Baptist in the last days of Herod the king; through the public ministry, death and resurrection of Jesus; into a second volume describing the birth of Christianity and its spread to the Gentiles; ending with Paul's imprisonment in Rome c. A.D. 62. If there are shortcomings in Luke's history—for example, his lack of chronological markers at every point—then we must judge him not by modern standards but by those of his era. By those canons Luke was an exceptional historian. Many noted ancient historians have given Luke high praise, including those who are not Christians. Luke is the most important historical contributor to the New Testament on account of the great span of years he narrates.

WORLD HISTORY AND SMALL MOVEMENTS

Evidence from Greco-Roman antiquity, in which the New Testament was written, is fragmentary and generally devoted to "important" people and events. Ancient studies are sure-footed in their inquiries into high profile people like emperors and kings. Their respective chronologies, policies and achievements are understood. Accordingly, when information about lesser people or movements comes to light, a context and environment is at hand in which to locate the smaller thing.

There are several exceptions to this generalization. One is the Qumran movement. The cache of texts discovered in 1947 near the northwest shore of the Dead Sea and the subsequent excavations uncovering the remains of a settlement nearby created great excitement. These discoveries provide a contemporary window into a small and "unimportant" Jewish sect that occupied the site for about two centuries but left otherwise small imprints in the histories of the day that have come down to us (mainly in Josephus).

Another small movement, at least at its beginnings, was the "sect of the Nazarenes" (Acts 24:5) in Jerusalem in the thirties of the first century. Like the Qumraners the early Christians were also known (sparsely) from external sources. Josephus and Tacitus refer to a movement begun in Jesus' day that was current in their own times decades later (see pp. 25-26 below). Unlike the Qumraners, however, the early Christians survived the dangers of history that might just as easily have destroyed them.

One matter on which an external source from "world history" (Tacitus) and internal sources (Paul and Acts) agree is that the birth of Christianity occurred as a burst of energy soon after Jesus' death. Tacitus states that following Pilate's execution of Christ the "pernicious superstition *broke out afresh* in Judaea" (*Annals* 15.44).

"World history" (about "important" people) is important since it provides a more or less stable context into which "unimportant" movements like the Qumraners and the early Christians can be located.

The preoccupation with "important" people is one reason "world history" has so little to say about Jesus. Had he led a military rebellion against the Romans, like Judas the Galilean in A.D. 6, Jesus may have left a greater imprint in history. But a harmless Jewish rabbi from a distant minor province accompanied by only twelve followers, who met his death by crucifixion, would not inspire much interest among the history writers of that day.

HISTORY IN THE NEW TESTAMENT

Our argument throughout is that Jesus and the first Christians are genuine figures of history and that they are faithfully and truthfully written about in the Gospels and Acts of the Apostles. These documents were written close in time to the events. They are historical and geographical in character. I am convinced that we are able to read these texts assured of their integrity and authenticity. At the same time, it would be unreasonable to measure them by modern canons of history writing. They are good products of their age and take their place with the best historical writing of that era, in particular the works of Luke in his Gospel and book of Acts.

The remainder of the New Testament consists of Letters, which are doctrinal and practical in nature rather than narratives. Yet even here we have a writer and readers, time and place. So even the Letters of the New Testament (including the Revelation, which is cast in letter format) are historical.

FURTHER READING

Edward Hallett Carr, *What Is History?* (New York: Knopf, 1962).

G. R. Elton, *The Practice of History,* 2nd ed. (Malden, Mass.: Blackwell Publishers, 2002).

Richard J. Evans, *In Defense of History* (New York: W. W. Norton, 1999).

2

THE QUESTION
OF TRUTH

In the year A.D. 135 after a three-year war, the Romans captured and beheaded the leader of a major Jewish uprising in which more than half a million Jews were killed, fifty fortresses destroyed and almost a thousand villages razed. This man, who called himself "President of Israel" and issued coins and land deeds as such, was hailed as the Messiah by the leading rabbi of the day. A formidable generalissimo who amputated a finger from each serving soldier, he was removed, according to the Roman emperor Hadrian, only by an "act of God." And yet, though this man was so great a figure, little evidence from the period has come to us, and such as there is does not even accurately record his name. His real name, ben Kosiba, has been known outside his own generation only since 1951, when some personal letters were discovered in a cave near the Dead Sea.

Almost exactly a century before ben Kosiba, the Romans had executed another Jew who had also been active in public for about three years. He had only twelve close followers, and he neither minted coins nor issued land deeds. But within a generation after his death his name was known outside Palestine, and within three centuries his symbol was inscribed on the shields of the soldiers of the Roman emperor Constantine and also on his coinage. Few parts of the world today have not heard the name of Jesus (even if only in blasphemy!). Millions of people claim to be his followers. Ben Kosiba and Jesus—quite a contrast, and one to which we shall return.

This book is written for people with questions about the historical reliability of the New Testament—questions like

- How close in time are the documents to Jesus?
- Can we believe the writings of the "biased" early Christians?
- Were any of the writers of the New Testament books eyewitnesses?
- Can we know if what was originally written has escaped alteration down through the centuries?
- Do we have any information apart from Christian sources?

THREE IMPORTANT PRELIMINARIES

First, please notice that our subject is not the *theological* but the *historical* reliability of the New Testament. These two aspects of reliability dovetail together into one total concept of reliability. They are inseparable really since the theology of the New Testament depends on the events concerning Jesus actually having taken place, and the events concerning Jesus are themselves profoundly theological. Nevertheless, this book will concentrate on the historical question.

Since the emphasis will be on history, on events, our area of investigation will be limited to the Gospels, the Acts of the Apostles and the relatively few autobiographical or historical sections of Paul's letters.

If the Gospels and Acts are historical as well as theological, how historical are they? Like other historical work in the ancient world, the Gospels and Acts differ from the writing of twentieth-century historians which is immensely detailed, with each statement supported by a reference. It would be unfair, however, to reject ancient histories like the Gospels and Acts because they do not conform to modern conventions of history writing. The writers of the Gospels and Acts supply facts, many facts, but not as comprehensively or elaborately as some modern authors. The biblical history writers have given their readers sufficient evidence on which to base a valid response to Jesus, but probably it isn't possible, from the information they have given, to rewrite the Gospels and Acts as precise modern histories. This, however, would be an unreasonable demand and one that could not be fairly made of Josephus or Tacitus or any other historical writer of the same period.

While, as we have stated, the New Testament does not assume the form of a history or a biography, being primarily concerned with Christian beliefs and behavior, nevertheless it rests on a foundation of facts. Many historical and biographical details are supplied which allow the historian to make a reasonable and coherent reconstruction, even if it is not complete in every respect. We may take it that the historical information contained in the New Testament is at least as accurate as that in other sources of the same period upon which modern historians depend when writing biographies of, say, Julius Caesar or King Herod the Great.

It may come as a surprise to us how professional many writers of that age were, even though they lacked modern tools such as computers and good maps. Those authors, including New Testament authors, certainly knew the difference between history and legend.[1] It would be utterly fallacious to believe, for example, that the New Testament story about King Herod the Great was like the story of King Arthur. Because of the extent, soberness, diversity and basic agreement of the available sources of information, the account of Herod can be accepted with considerable confidence. On the other hand, the information about Arthur comes from legends and romantic stories and in so many differing versions as to make doubtful the very existence of Arthur. The information we have about Jesus, Peter and Paul was recorded close in time to the events related and is sufficiently confirmed for the historicity of Jesus, Peter and Paul to be put in the same general class as, for example, that of Caesar or Herod.

Second, what I have to say about the historical accuracy of the New Testament does not require the reader's acceptance of it as part of the inspired Word of God. That is a view you may come to, as I have. However, it would be unreasonable to expect the as-yet unconvinced reader to adopt this belief, nor is it my intention here to argue that case, which is a question of theology.[2] When you have finished this book you may say that you now believe that the documents of the New Testament have a definite historical aspect, and that they are essentially reliable. I do not expect you to say that you now believe it is the Word of God, and therefore will confine my comments to those matters that can be checked as historical fact, or for which a case of probability can be argued. You will not be expected to accept anything in this book "by faith." What I will attempt to present is an objectively reasoned case, the details of which will be open to further inquiry.

Third, it will be helpful if we also keep in mind the fact that what is now called the New Testament originally consisted of twenty-seven separate scrolls of varying length. Matthew, for example, would have been written on a papyrus scroll about thirty-three feet long. Those twenty-seven scrolls were written by Matthew; Mark; Luke (Gospel and Acts); John (Gospel, Letters, perhaps Revelation); Paul; the author of Hebrews; James; Peter and Jude—nine authors in all, ten if Revelation was by a different John. It is vital to understand that most of the authors wrote independently of one another, and that their scrolls circulated separately until the second century.

With the passage of time and the growth of new congregations, the copies of the original scrolls were gathered together for reading in church. Although Christian writers of the second and third centuries list the documents that were in use in the churches, the list of books of the New Testament as we have them today was not formalized until late in the fourth century by the Councils of Hippo Regius and Carthage in North Africa. F. F. Bruce comments: "What these [ecclesiastical] councils did was not to impose something new upon the Christian communities but to codify what was already the general practice of those communities."[3]

A MAJOR OBSTACLE

But how sure can we be about people and events so long ago? To many people this is a major obstacle barring the path to further inquiry about Jesus. Why couldn't he have lived closer to our own time? Two comments may be offered.

Part of the difficulty is a mathematical illusion. Two thousand years seems such a vast expanse of time. But what if we measured the period since the birth of Jesus by individual life spans? If we take the average life span to be about seventy years, it would require no more than thirty such life spans to bring us back to New Testament times. The first would take us to the rise of Hitler and World War II, the second to the Civil War, the third to the presidency of George Washington and so on. The thirtieth would take us to the birth of Jesus. Measured in years the two-thousand-year period is hard to comprehend, but it's not as hard to grasp in terms of individual life spans.

Another problem for us is to think of history in neat progressive terms.

Old means primitive; recent means developed. While this may be true of history overall, it is by no means true that the tenth century is an exact mid-point in terms of progress between Jesus in the first century and our generation in the twenty-first. In many ways the first century, when Greco-Roman society was at its height, was more civilized than the Middle or Dark Ages. In fact, we know more about the Roman emperor Augustus than about the eleventh-century English king Harold, even though the latter is a thousand years closer to us than the former. It is fortunate for the study of Christian origins that Jesus was born in such a literate, well-documented period.

Let me conclude this chapter on a personal note. As a young adult, what I found compelling about Christianity was the sense of gratitude associated with the forgiveness of sins through the death of Christ. Christianity was "true" for me in a personal way, and I accepted that it was as true objectively or historically as my new Christian friends assured me it was, but without real confidence.

Some time later I entered theological college to train for the ministry. While some attention was given to questions of history and truth, most of my time there was devoted to the study of Greek and Hebrew, to the intensive exegesis of the literature of the Bible and to systematic theology. A good foundation of theological knowledge was laid, but the history question was (for me) still up in the air.

It was only later, when I studied ancient history at the university level, that the matter was finally settled in my mind. In the course of three years of Roman and Greek history and Greek language I came to appreciate how solid the evidence for Christianity was, relative to other great people and movements in antiquity. It wasn't that our courses investigated Christianity; quite the reverse. In fact, Jesus was only once or twice referred to in the many lectures on ancient history I attended while in college. What I discovered, though, was that the historical evidence for Jesus and the origins of Christianity compared favorably with that available for Tiberius, the Roman emperor in whose time Jesus exercised his ministry, or for Alexander the Great or the emperor Nero.

This book is written from the conviction that there is a sound historical basis to the New Testament. What it attempts to do is to place the evidence before the reader for examination. Let the evidence speak for itself and lead where it will.

FURTHER READING

C. H. Dodd, *The Founder of Christianity* (New York: Macmillan, 1970).

David Brian Winter, *The Search for the Real Jesus* (Wilton, Conn.: Morehouse, 1982).

Yigael Yadin, *Bar-Kokhba* (London: Random House, 1971).

DID JESUS EXIST?

Early Non-Christian References

As we have seen, the book we call the New Testament is a slim collection of writings made up of twenty-seven pieces of varying length written by nine or ten different authors, all of them convinced Christians. That's fine if you are already a Christian. But what if you're not? Are you expected to make up your mind about Jesus just on the say-so of nine or ten biased Christians who wrote the New Testament? It would be rather like having to reach a decision about Karl Marx based entirely on what Marxists say about him.

And what if Jesus never existed anyway? Many people have wondered about that, and the thought has crossed my own mind more than once. Perhaps he was a figment of the imagination of those early Christians? This opinion has been periodically expressed in a serious way, most recently by George Albert Wells, a professor of German who in 1971 wrote a book titled *The Jesus of the Early Christians.*

Despite their admitted bias, I hope to show that the New Testament writers themselves are the best reason for believing the existence of Jesus. However, as it happens, there is other early information about Jesus written by non-Christians. These non-Christian sources fall into two broad classes, Roman and Jewish.

ROMAN SOURCES

Pliny: Letters from Bithynia c. A.D. 110. In about A.D. 110 the emperor Trajan sent Pliny (A.D. 61-113), an experienced administrator, to be governor of the disorderly province of Bithynia, south of the Black Sea. A few years later Pliny wrote to the emperor seeking advice about a troublesome group known as "Christians." An unsigned paper giving the names of many Christians had been given to the governor, who had put them in prison. But how was he to conduct the trial? What punishments were appropriate? Should the young be punished as severely as the old? Would renunciation of Jesus earn pardon? Pliny wrote to Emperor Trajan for advice on these and similar questions.

The Christian movement had taken quite a hold in the region. Pliny complained to Trajan that "*many* of all ages and every rank and also of both sexes" were involved and, like a spreading disease, "not the cities only, but also the villages and the country" were affected. The new movement had become so powerful that the temples were deserted and those who sold food for the animal sacrifices had not been able to find buyers. Pliny's letter reveals that this movement was not altogether new, since some of the prisoners whom he threatened said that they had given up being Christians twenty years earlier. We conclude that there must have been Christians in Bithynia at least by the late eighties of the first century A.D., perhaps earlier. Peter's first letter, written in the early sixties, is addressed to Christians in Bithynia (among others), thus confirming what we learn from Pliny.

Who were these "Christians" and what did they believe? Pliny interrogated them and told Trajan:

> They maintained, however, that the amount of their fault or error had been this, that it was their habit on a fixed day to assemble before daylight and recite by turns a form of words to Christ as a god; and that they bound themselves with an oath, not for any crime, but not to commit theft or robbery or adultery, not to break their word, and not to deny a deposit when demanded. After this was done, their custom was to depart, and to meet again to take food, but ordinary and harmless food.[1]

Pliny's comments are the earliest surviving non-Christian description of what Christians believed and how they lived. What is of greatest interest is that these people regarded Christ as a god (or as God). They did not venerate him as a deceased martyr but agreed together by a form of words that he was a divine figure, in some way their living contemporary.

There is no reason to believe that their attitude to Jesus was a recent development. Half a century earlier Peter had reminded the Christians of Bithynia (and others) that, "Through him [that is, Christ] you believe in God, who raised him from the dead and glorified him" (1 Pet 1:21 NIV).

Without knowing it, Pliny confirms as historically accurate some details found in the New Testament.

First, he confirms that early Christianity sometimes destroyed the business side of the older religions. Like the shrine makers in Ephesus (Acts 19:24-41), the suppliers of food for sacrificial animals in Bithynia were put out of business by the impact of the Christian movement.

Second, Pliny mentions that Christians met for worship on a "fixed day." This can be compared with the meeting in Troas on the "first day of the week" to "break bread" (Acts 20:7), which probably refers to the holy Communion.

Third, Pliny states that the Christians prayed to Jesus as God (or as a god) while refusing to curse him. This confirms as accurate Paul's statement that "no one speaking by the Spirit of God ever says 'Jesus be cursed!' and no one can say 'Jesus is Lord' except by the Holy Spirit" (1 Cor 12:3).

This encourages us to believe, at least in these three references, that the biblical account is true. Based on what Pliny wrote there can be no doubt about the existence in about A.D. 110 of a substantial body of Christians in remote Bithynia. This is a fact of history. But how do we explain this fact? How did they come to be there? Their presence was a historical *effect* for which there was some *cause*. What was it?

Christian inscription in Pompeii. Seven examples of the following inscription have been found, including two in Pompeii that were sealed in volcanic ash by the eruption of Mount Vesuvius in A.D. 79.

R	O	T	A	S
O	P	E	R	A
T	E	N	E	T
A	R	E	P	O
S	A	T	O	R

The reconstruction that is accepted by many indicates that the inscription is Christian. The letters in the square can be redistributed, with none spare, to make two *A*s, two *O*s and the word *PATERNOSTER* (Latin: "Our Father") in both arms of a cross.

```
                          A
                          P
                          A
                          T
                          E
                          R
            A  PATERNOSTER  O
                          O
                          S
                          T
                          E
                          R
                          O
```

A and *O* stand for the Greek letters alpha and omega, symbols for God in Revelation 1:8, 21:6 and 22:13. If this is a correct understanding it means that there were Christians in Pompeii by the seventies. This should cause no surprise, given the large Christian community in nearby Rome in the sixties, as attested by Tacitus.[2]

Tacitus: Writing about the fire in Rome in A.D. 64. Tacitus (A.D. 55-c.120) was made governor of the province of Asia soon after Pliny's appointment to Bithynia, and something of his reputation as a historian may be discerned in part of the letter written to him by his friend Pliny:

> Thank you for asking me to send you a description of my uncle's death so that you can leave an accurate account of it for posterity. . . . I know that immortal fame awaits him if his death is recorded by you. (*Epistles* 6.16)

In his *Annals of Imperial Rome* written at about the same time as Pliny wrote the above letter, Tacitus describes how the emperor Nero attempted to divert blame from himself to a new and detested religious sect for lighting the fire that destroyed three-quarters of Rome:

But all human efforts, all the lavish gifts of the emperor, and the propitiations of the gods, did not banish the sinister belief that the conflagration was the result of an order. Consequently, to get rid of the report, Nero fastened the guilt and inflicted the most exquisite tortures on a class hated for their abominations, called Christians by the populace. Christus, from whom the name had its origin, suffered the extreme penalty during the reign of Tiberius at the hands of one of our procurators, Pontius Pilate, and a deadly superstition, thus checked for the moment, again broke out not only in Judaea, the first source of the evil, but also in the City [Rome], where all things hideous and shameful from every part of the world meet and become popular. Accordingly, an arrest was first made of all who confessed; then, upon their information, an immense multitude was convicted, not so much of the crime of arson, as of hatred of the human race. (*Annals* 15.44.2-5)

It appears that Tacitus, like Pliny, despised but perhaps also feared this new movement. He describes the Christians as "a class hated for their abominations . . . a deadly superstition . . . evil . . . hideous . . . shameful." He accuses them of "hatred of the human race," which may refer to the Christian refusal to acknowledge Caesar as a god and the Roman state as divine.

In one sentence from the above passage Tacitus confirms six details mentioned in the New Testament:

1. The public career of Christ occurred in the time of the emperor Tiberius (Lk 3:1).
2. Pontius Pilate was the Roman governor when Christ died (Mt 27:2; Mk 15:1; Luke 23:1; Acts 3:13 and 13:28).
3. Christ was executed as a criminal (Lk 23:2).
4. This occurred in Judea (Mk 11:16).
5. The movement did not die with Jesus, but "broke out" again.
6. The movement spread from Jerusalem to Rome (Acts 1:4 and 28:14).

This sentence agrees, in a broad sense, with the geographic sweep of Luke-Acts, a two-volume work that begins with Jesus in Judea (Lk 2:4) and ends with Paul in Rome (Acts 28:14). Tacitus confirms both the existence of Christ and the spread of early Christianity.

This raises the question of why authors such as Pliny and Tacitus fail to say more about Jesus himself. In attempting an answer, we must stand in the shoes of these men. It is well to remember that both were from the upper strata of Roman society and therefore very conservative. Aristocratic Romans were backward looking; they venerated Rome's illustrious past history, culture and institutions. They disliked change, especially when it came from non-Roman quarters such as Judea. This is why Pliny and Tacitus both despised and feared the virulent new movement. It was a foreign superstition that was rapidly spreading like a disease across the Empire. Perhaps Tacitus's reference to Christians in Rome as an "immense multitude" on one hand, or Pliny's of Christians in Bithynia as "a multitude of men" on the other, are exaggerations—propaganda to scare people.

Here the evidence from the New Testament provides confirmation of the astonishing spread of the new movement. In A.D. 50 Paul's opponents in Macedonia complain, "These men . . . have turned the world upside down" (Acts 17:6), while in A.D. 62 the Jews in Rome ask the apostle about "this sect . . . that everywhere . . . is spoken against" (Acts 28:22). The fears of Pliny and Tacitus were well grounded. Less than a century from the time they wrote, the Christian apologist Tertullian could claim:

> We are but of yesterday, and we have filled everything you have—cities, tenements, forts, towns . . . even the camps, tribes, palace, senate, forum. All we have left to you are the temples. (*Apology* 37.4)

What Pliny and Tacitus described was a movement several decades old, but which was by then worldwide and spreading rapidly. Inevitably it came to the attention of the writers of that time, though it is worth noticing that only part of the literature of the period has survived. But if a threatening movement was noticed by the Roman writers, a man on his own was not, especially if that man was a *crucified* Jew. Cicero, the Roman lawyer who lived before Christ, wrote:

> Even the mere word, *cross*, must remain far not only from the lips of the citizens of Rome, but also from their thoughts, their eyes, their ears. (*Pro Rabirio* 5.16)

The reason Roman historians remain relatively silent about Jesus himself may be that crucifixion was unmentionable. Perhaps this is why Tacitus in another work, when reviewing the history of Judea at the time of Jesus, said "under Tiberius all was quiet" (*History* 5.9).

Suetonius: Writing about Rome c. A.D. 49. Suetonius (A.D. 69-c.140), in common with the other Roman writers, writes damningly of the Christians. He speaks of them as "a class of man given to a new and wicked superstition" (*Life of Nero* 16.2). "Class" suggests a group that was numerically significant while "new and wicked superstition" conveys the revulsion many educated Romans felt toward the Christians.

In what is probably a reference to Christ, Suetonius relates an incident in the year A.D. 49: "Since the Jews constantly made disturbances at the instigation of Chrestus, he [Claudius] expelled them from Rome" (*Life of Claudius* 25.4; cf. Acts 18:2). If by "Chrestus" Suetonius is referring to Jesus "Christus," as most scholars believe, it means that there were Christians in Rome by A.D. 49. But this is only to corroborate what the Christian sources tell us.

When Paul arrived in Italy about A.D. 60, he met Christians at Puteoli in the south (Acts 28:13) and was welcomed by an advance party even before he reached Rome (Acts 28:15). About three years earlier he had written his magnum opus, the *Letter to the Romans*, which virtually demanded the existence of a Christian community of some size to warrant the effort. He told them that their "faith is proclaimed in all the world" (Rom 1:8) and that he had often "intended to come" to them (Rom 1:13; 15:22-24). Clearly the presence of Christians in Rome predates the letter by some years.

In A.D. 49 the emperor Claudius expelled the Jews from Rome because of problems caused by Christianity. Among them were Aquila and Priscilla, who settled in Corinth and who were almost certainly Christians (see Acts 18:2-3). If Aquila and Priscilla were in fact Christians, it is quite possible that they were involved in the disturbances about "Chrestus" that led to the mass expulsion of the Jews from Rome.

If there were Christians in Italy by the late forties, how did they come to be there? One thing that can be said is that, despite later church tradition, Peter or Paul did not introduce the movement. Peter was still in Palestine in the late forties (Gal 2:11), and Paul did not arrive in Rome until the early sixties (Acts 28:14). While the two apostles may have helped to stabilize an already existing Christian community, its origin is probably due to the migration of Christian Jews from Judea in the thirties and forties.

How large a movement was early Christianity? What do these Roman writers tell us?

The non-Christian sources, supported and supplemented by Christian sources, indicate the presence of Christians in Bithynia within the period c. 64-110 and in Rome c. 49-64. What is striking is the *number* of Christians involved. Pliny wrote of "many of all ages and every rank . . . from . . . not the cities only, but also villages and the country" whose presence had destroyed the ancient religions in Bithynia. This is a major movement. In writing of Claudius expelling all the Jews from Rome in A.D. 49 "at the instigation of Chrestus" we may take it that Suetonius is implying that the disturbances were of a most serious kind if they warranted the expulsion of many Jews from the city. Fifteen years later (A.D. 64), when fire destroyed three-quarters of the world capital and a suitable scapegoat was sought and found in the "class . . . called Christians," the implication again is that they must have been of a significant number. There would be no point in blaming a small or unknown group.

Although we cannot explain precisely how Christianity came to Bithynia or Rome, we can say that it originated with Jesus in Judea. Who he was and what he did in Judea, the epicenter, went unrecorded by Roman writers of the time. Nevertheless extensive shock waves rolled to the farthest shores of the Mediterranean world that in time left their marks in the records. The writers may have failed to take account of Jesus, the cause of it all, but they could hardly ignore the effects.

JEWISH SOURCES

Benediction Twelve. After the disastrous war with the Romans from A.D. 66 to 70, the Jewish Sanhedrin (or Senate), ceased to exist as a political and administrative body. The emperor Vespasian brought Judea under direct military rule, leaving the Sanhedrin with a purely religious role. Most of the sects and parties within Judaism perished with the war. Two that survived were the Pharisees, representing the mainstream of Jewish religious life, and the

Nazarenes, or Christians, who by then were regarded as heretical. In the eighties the Pharisee-dominated Sanhedrin meeting at Jamnia, a town to the east of Jerusalem, formulated the following synagogue prayer:

> For the renegades let there be no hope, and may the arrogant kingdom soon be rooted out in our days, and the Nazarenes and the minim perish as in a moment and be blotted out from the book of life and with the righteous may they not be inscribed. Blessed art thou, O Lord, who humblest the arrogant.[3]

References in the Talmud indicate that the "minim" and the "Nazarenes" usually refer to Christians. This bitter prayer clearly attests the existence of Christians in Judea in the post-70 period, and it represents a tragic contrast with the frequently happy relations of Christian Jews with their fellow Jews in the period before the war. From Christian sources we read of Jewish Christian priests (Acts 6:7) and Christian Pharisees (Acts 15:5) and of "many thousands . . . among the Jews . . . who have believed . . . all zealous for the law" (Acts 21:20). Opposition there may have been from Sadducean high priests (Acts 4:1-3) and Herod Agrippa (Acts 12:1-3), but the Pharisees appear either to have been neutral, as was Rabbi Gamaliel (Acts 5:34-39), or well-disposed like those who protested at the unjust death of James brother of Jesus (Josephus *Antiquities* 20.197-203). The grim sentiments of *Benediction Twelve* reflect the thorough separation of synagogue and church after the end of the war in A.D. 70.

The Talmud. The Talmuds were compiled in Jerusalem and Babylon in the fifth and sixth centuries. Their late dating raises questions as to the authenticity of references to Jesus. Of various possibilities the most likely mention of Jesus is this:

> It was taught: On the day before the Passover they hanged Jesus. A herald went before him for forty days [proclaiming]. "He will be stoned, because he practised magic and enticed Israel to go astray. Let anyone who knows anything in his favour come forward and plead for him." But nothing was found in his favour, and they hanged him the day before Passover. (*b. Sanhedrin* 43a)

This rather bitter reference is more likely to have arisen in the centuries after Jesus than closer to his times. We note the apologetic detail that since no one defended him he must have been guilty. Here Jesus is a magician and a deceiver of the nation and for this the Jews executed him. According to the Gospels and Tacitus (*Annals* 15.44), however, the Romans executed Jesus for treasonably claiming to be "king of the Jews." Apart from the timing of his death to the Passover season there is little else here that coincides with other information at hand, including the manner of his death by hanging.

Josephus. Josephus, an aristocratic Pharisee, was born in A.D. 37. During the war with the Romans from A.D. 66 to 70, he was captured by the Romans and later was paid a pension by successive emperors for services rendered to the imperial family. Early in the nineties he wrote the *Jewish Antiquities*.

Pharisees were not always bitterly opposed to Christians, as the Jewish historian clearly shows. Before the war, in an interregnum between Roman governors (A.D. 62), the high priest Annas (son of Annas of the Gospels)

> convened the judges of the Sanhedrin and brought before them a man named James, the brother of Jesus who was called the Christ, and certain others. He accused them of having transgressed the law and delivered them up to be stoned. Those of the inhabitants of the city who were considered the most fair-minded and who were strict in observance of the law were offended at this. (*Antiquities* 20.197-203)

Those who were "strict in observance of the law" must refer to Pharisees, which suggests they showed a degree of sympathy to James, brother of Jesus, who was leader of the multitudinous Jerusalem church. The members of that church, Paul had been informed, were "all zealous for the law" (Acts 21:20), which explains why the Pharisees were favorably disposed towards James. James's reference to "many thousands" of such Jerusalem believers (Acts 21:20), while possibly an exaggeration, nevertheless confirms the impression given elsewhere of large numbers of people involved in Christianity, and that it was a worldwide movement.

In this extract, the authenticity of which is not in doubt, Josephus confirms two important pieces of information from the New Testament.

1. Jesus was "called Christ" (cf. Acts 2:36).

2. James was his brother (cf. Gal 1:19).

Josephus indicates no doubt as to the genuine existence in history of either Jesus or James.

Disputed cases. Josephus refers to Jesus earlier in his *Antiquities* in a passage that is known to scholars as the *Testimonium Flavianum*:

> About that time there lived Jesus, a wise man, if indeed one ought to call him a man. For he was one who wrought surprising feats and was a teacher of such people as accept the truth gladly. He won over many Jews and many of the Greeks. He was the Messiah. When Pilate, upon hearing him accused by men of the highest standing among us, had condemned him to be crucified, those who had in the first place come to love him did not give up their affection for him. On the third day he appeared to them restored to life, for the prophets of God had prophesied these and countless other marvelous things about him. And the tribe of the Christians so called after him, has still to this day not disappeared. (*Antiquities* 18.63-64)

While this passage is in all the extant manuscripts of the *Antiquities* and is externally attested by church historian Eusebius, who quoted it exactly and in full in A.D. 325, there are many who question its authenticity. The major problem is that another Christian writer, Origen, writing a century earlier than Eusebius, remarked in passing that Josephus "did not believe in Jesus as the Christ" (*Against Celsus* 1.47). This apparently contradicts the text as it stands. It may be that some zealous but misguided Christian has tampered with the text, removing the phrase "so-called" before Christ, as in the passage referring to the death of James. If the text were amended along those lines it would make sense of Origen's comment. Another problem is the expression "if it is possible to call him a man." Is this another Christian interpolation, reflecting the orthodox doctrine of the deity of Christ, or was it a piece of mild sarcasm by Josephus, knowing that deity claims were made for Jesus?

Those two problems apart, many scholars are prepared to accept much or all of the remainder of the text as genuine. I am impressed by the reference to the Christians as not being extinct "to this day" which echoes the same laissez-faire neutrality toward Christianity as shown by Josephus's fellow Pharisee Gamaliel back in the thirties (Acts 5:38-39). Also, I detect in Josephus's words, "wrought surprising feats . . . a teacher" an echo of yet another Pharisee, Nicodemus, who said that Jesus was a "teacher" who performed "signs" (Jn 3:2). Josephus's reference to Jesus as "teacher" and miracle worker is close to Nicodemus's address to Jesus as "teacher" and "miracle" worker.

Finally the phrase "a wise man" is a favorable variation of "a charlatan man," a phrase used repeatedly for the turbulent would-be miracle-working prophets whom Josephus vilifies elsewhere in his writings. Since Jesus was a nonviolent, nonpolitical miracle worker and teacher, Josephus might well refer to him as "a wise man." Rather than reject this extract altogether, it seems preferable to accept it with some deletions. In broad terms it confirms and amplifies the comments of Tacitus.

A third uncertain case is the recently discovered letter written by the Jewish revolutionary leader, ben Kosiba. The writer speaks menacingly of "the Galileans," which is believed by many to mean "the Christians." Here is the letter in full:

> From Shimeon ben Kosiba to Yeshua ben Galoula and to the men of the fort, peace. I take heaven to witness against me that unless you mobilize [destroy?] the Galileans who are with you, every man, I will put fetters on your feet as I did to ben Aphlul.[4]

Yigael Yadin, who discovered the letter in a cave near the Dead Sea, rejects the suggestion that "Galileans" means Christians. Ben Kosiba, however, is known from other sources to have persecuted Christians. The Christian writer Justin Martyr, a contemporary of ben Kosiba, commented:

> In the present Jewish war it was only Christians whom bar Chocheba [another name for Kosiba], the leader of the rebellion of the Jews, commanded to be punished severely if they did not deny Jesus as the messiah of the Jews and blaspheme him.[5]

Most likely these were Christian Jews who, in their loyalty to Jesus, apparently refused to recognize ben Kosiba as Messiah. They may also have declined to take part in the uprising, following the example of the Jerusalem church whose members withdrew from the war zone during the first Jewish war in A.D. 66-70. Thus ben Kosiba had two reasons to punish the Christians: they did not recognize him, and they refused to fight in his war. Ben Kosiba's reference to "Galileans" may well refer to Christians.

SUMMARY OF THE NON-CHRISTIAN EVIDENCE

On the basis of this evidence from non-Christian sources, it is possible to draw the following conclusions:

1. Jesus Christ was executed (by crucifixion?) in Judea during the period when Tiberius was emperor (A.D. 14-37) and Pontius Pilate was governor (A.D. 26-36). *Tacitus*

2. The movement spread from Judea to Rome. *Tacitus*

3. His followers worshiped him as (a) god. *Pliny*

4. He was called "the Christ." *Josephus*

5. His followers were called "Christians." *Tacitus, Pliny*

6. They were numerous in Bithynia and Rome. *Tacitus, Pliny*

7. His brother was James. *Josephus*

While this evidence is not extensive, it is noteworthy that it does not in any way conflict with, but rather confirms, the historical information in the New Testament.

FURTHER READING

F. F. Bruce, *Jesus and Christian Origins Outside the New Testament* (Grand Rapids: Eerdmans, 1974).

Howard Clark Kee, *Jesus in History* (San Diego: Harcourt Brace & World, 1977).

Robert Van Voorst, *Jesus Outside the New Testament* (Grand Rapids: Eerdmans, 2000).

FIXING THE TIME FRAME

A useful as the nonbiblical information is in establishing that Jesus really lived, the evidence of the New Testament is both earlier and more extensive.

"But," you say, "I cannot be expected to believe that. The New Testament was all written by Christians." This is an understandable reaction and I can sympathize with it. But let me make two comments.

First, the holding of personal convictions doesn't necessarily mean blindness or dishonesty. A biographer may admire a statesman so much that he goes to the trouble to research and write about him. If the writer is competent and well-balanced he will not omit the shortcomings and failures of his subject. Admiration may be the motive in writing, but it does not destroy objectivity; this depends on the integrity of the writer. Luke admired Paul and was his friend, yet he does not conceal the quarrel between Paul and Barnabas nor Paul's questionable reaction when struck at the command of the high priest (Acts 15:36-41; 23:3). Mark was a convinced follower of Jesus, and yet he doesn't omit the cursing of the fig tree (Mk 11:12-14), an incident that has troubled many people. Similarly John, the beloved disciple, records Jesus speaking to his mother in what appears to be a harsh way (Jn 2:4). In fact, the presence in the New Testament of details that we find awkward points to realism and honesty by the apostolic writers.

Second, the New Testament did not always exist as a single volume. Some people believe that the apostles called a meeting and decided who would write which part—"Matthew, Mark, Luke, John, you each write a Gospel

and Paul, you write some letters. And let us put it all together in one book."
Let me say, quite definitely, that the books of the New Testament were not
written and collected like that.

Paul wrote to the Galatians because they were getting away from the gospel message. The Corinthians had some practical problems that they listed
in a letter to Paul; 1 Corinthians is his answer to these and other matters.
Mark was written to set down information about Jesus in a more permanent
form and also to bring the good news about Jesus to a particular group of
readers, probably Greek-speaking Romans. People hermetically sealed off
from life did not write the books of the New Testament; quite the opposite
in fact. Every part of the New Testament, as far as I can see, is a response to
real life needs. It is a collection of "occasional" literature, each part written
for some specific occasion or purpose.

Moreover, the New Testament writers were not in league with each other
at the point of writing. Nothing Mark wrote indicates any verbal influence
by Paul, or vice versa. John did not depend on Paul nor, many scholars believe, upon Mark. While Luke and Matthew have used Mark, their Gospels
appear to have been written independently of each other and of John. While
James, Hebrews and 1 Peter hold some ideas in common with Paul, none of
them appears to have been influenced by, or to be dependent upon, any
other. This literary independence reflects the fact that the writers were active
missionaries whose spheres of work were both specialized in themselves
and, to a significant degree, remote from one another.

Further, it is quite certain that the literature was not collected into a single
volume quickly, but over a considerable period of time. Paul wrote to the
Colossians and the Laodiceans (whose letter has been lost) requesting that
the letters be exchanged and read in both churches (Col 4:16). We may assume that the churches copied the originals for rereading and also exchanged letters with one another. But it took many years before the books
of the New Testament were widely circulated and collected.

The New Testament existed in the first place as many separate parts, written separately and circulated separately. The parts were only finally recognized as belonging to one official volume or "canon" in the fourth century,
though the principle of recognition existed from the earliest times. Because

the parts were produced separately and independently, we have a number of built-in means of checking one against the other. Since there are seven or eight independently written accounts that refer to Jesus, it is as reasonable to believe he existed as it is to believe a road accident happened because seven or eight people independently said it did. The evidence for Christ is to be accepted or rejected in much the same way a judge and jury accept or reject evidence from witnesses to an accident or a crime.

FIXING THE TIME FRAME OF PAUL'S LETTERS

The time frame of the missionary career of Paul can be fixed with great confidence. When Paul arrived in Corinth, he met Aquila and Priscilla who had recently "come from Italy . . . because Claudius had commanded all the Jews to leave Rome" (Acts 18:2). This dovetails with the Roman historian Suetonius, who wrote that Claudius banished from Rome all Jews because they were continually making disturbances about Christ and Christianity (*Claudius* 25). Scholars of Roman history date this expulsion to c. A.D. 49. We conclude that Paul arrived in Corinth some time during A.D. 50. An inscription that fixes the beginning of Gallio's one-year appointment as proconsul in Achaia at July A.D. 51 confirms this, a detail that corresponds with the reference in Acts that "when Gallio was proconsul of Achaia, the Jews made a united attack upon Paul and brought him before the tribunal" (Acts 18:12). Since 1 Thessalonians, by common consent, was written from Corinth soon after Paul's arrival there (1 Thess 3:6 and Acts 18:5), we conclude that this letter was written in A.D. 50. This represents the earliest generally accepted extremity of the time frame. Few scholars dispute this date, although some may place Paul's letter to the Galatians earlier, about A.D. 48.

The other extremity of the time frame is fixed by the decision of Festus, Roman procurator of Judea, to dispatch Paul to Rome (Acts 25:12). Historians set the date for Festus's arrival in Judea at about A.D. 60. The author of Acts, who was with Paul, is quite specific. No more than two weeks after his arrival, Festus convened the hearing in which he decided to send Paul to be tried by Caesar (Acts 25:1-6). Paul's departure for Rome must have followed shortly after that (Acts 25:13, 23; 27:1). We conclude that Paul set out for Rome in A.D. 60 and after many adventures arrived some time early the next year (Acts 27:9, 27; 28:11-17). Acts concludes with a reference to Paul's two-year imprisonment in Rome, that is, in A.D. 61 and 62, during which time he probably wrote the letter to the Philippians (Phil 1:7, 13; 4:22).

The fourth-century Christian writer Eusebius states that Paul was executed in Rome under Nero (*Church History* 2:25). Since Nero died in A.D. 68, Paul's death obviously occurred sometime between A.D. 63 and A.D. 68, thereby setting the latter extremity of his letter writing.

Thus the time frame for Paul's letters is from about A.D. 50 to the middle-late sixties. Why am I making so much of the time frame for Paul's writings? Because it can be established with such complete confidence, and because it is so close in time to the life and death of Jesus of Nazareth. According to Tacitus, Jesus was executed in Judea in the time of Pontius Pilate who was governor from A.D. 26 to 36. Evidence from the Gospels and from calendar calculations has fixed the date of the crucifixion as either A.D. 30 or 33. If Jesus died in A.D. 33, as many believe, then a mere seventeen years separates that event from the widely agreed earliest of Paul's letters, 1 Thessalonians. In that letter Paul writes that "the Jews . . . killed . . . the Lord Jesus" (1 Thess 2:14-15). Based on the early evidence from Paul, there can be no reasonable doubt that Jesus was a genuine figure of history.

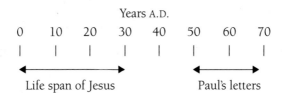

Years A.D.

0   10   20   30   40   50   60   70

Life span of Jesus   Paul's letters

FIXING THE TIME FRAME FOR THE REST OF THE NEW TESTAMENT

If we can "fix" Paul's writings to a particular period, what about the other fourteen parts of the New Testament, in particular the Gospels? Here we have a problem. We are able to establish a time frame for Paul because of the Acts of the Apostles and also because of such external milestones as Gallio's appointment in Achaia, the expulsion of the Jews from Rome and the arrival of Festus in Judea. But there is no documentary evidence external to the

Gospels that states when they were written, and the writers themselves do not say. The same is true of the remaining ten pieces of the New Testament.

In the absence of external documentary evidence, some scholars appeal to the evidence of events such as Nero's persecutions of Christians in Rome beginning in A.D. 64 and the devastating war in Palestine in A.D. 66-70 that culminated in the demolition of the temple in Jerusalem. These events were so momentous that, it is argued, they must have some echo within the New Testament. Thus it is suggested that 1 Peter must be dated shortly before A.D. 64 because of the references to impending persecution (1 Pet 1:6-7; 3:13-17; 4:12-19; 5:8-11). The references to high priests and sacrifices in the letter to the Hebrews (Heb 5:1-4; 10:11) have been taken to suggest that the temple was still in use and that the letter must accordingly be earlier than A.D. 70. With respect to the non-Pauline part of the New Testament, John A. T. Robinson has argued that the lack of any reference to the Jewish-Roman war A.D. in 66-70 may mean that every part of the New Testament was written beforehand.[1]

All that can be said in these matters, however, is that a case can be made but not proved. The problem is that the evidence is circumstantial and sometimes ambiguous. At this stage in New Testament study there is no consensus about the precise dating of the non-Pauline literature. In the absence of new evidence, New Testament scholars will continue to express different opinions about the dates.

Although no one can say exactly when the Gospels were written, we can say with certainty the dates by which they were in circulation. There is external documentary evidence by which we can fix the outer limits of the time frame.

The coming of Jesus and the activity of the apostles, spoken and written, sparked off an explosion of Christian literature in the second and third centuries. Three authors wrote close to the year 100—Clement in about 96, Ignatius in about 108 and Polycarp in about 110. What is significant for this discussion is that these writers quote from, or refer to, many books of the New Testament. In the first dozen sentences of Polycarp's letter to the Philippians, written in about 110, he quotes from Acts, 1 Peter, Ephesians and the Gospel of Matthew, thus establishing that these books were in use by the time he wrote. Altogether Polycarp[2] attests the existence of

Matthew	Acts	Romans	Hebrews
Mark		1 Corinthians	1 Peter
Luke		2 Corinthians	1 John
John		Galatians	
		Ephesians	
		Philippians	
		Colossians	
		2 Thessalonians	
		1 Timothy	
		2 Timothy	

In his seven short letters written c. 108, Ignatius[3] quotes or refers to

Matthew	Acts	Romans	Hebrews
Mark		1 Corinthians	James
Luke		2 Corinthians	1 Peter
John		Galatians	2 Peter
		Ephesians	1 John
		Philippians	3 John
		Colossians	Revelation
		1 Thessalonians	
		1 Timothy	
		2 Timothy	
		Titus	
		Philemon	

Clement,[4] writing from Rome to Corinth c. 96, refers to

Matthew	Romans	Hebrews
Mark	1 Corinthians	James
Luke	Ephesians	1 Peter
	1 Timothy	
	Titus	

On the basis of these three early Christian authors it can be stated that twenty-five pieces of the New Testament were definitely in circulation by about the year 100. By that date 1 Thessalonians had been in use for fifty years. The non-Pauline pieces quoted or referred to may have been in use for a comparable period, but unfortunately there is no way of knowing for certain. The point I am making is that attestation by Clement in c. 96 of, let's say, Mark does not imply that Mark was necessarily of recent composition. It could just as easily have been in circulation for three or four decades. The silence of Clement, Ignatius and Polycarp with respect to 2 John and Jude need not imply that these books were not written, only that those authors failed to quote from them or refer to them.

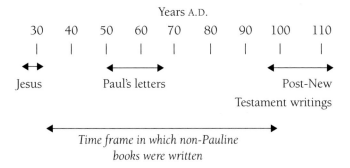

Years A.D.

| 30 | 40 | 50 | 60 | 70 | 80 | 90 | 100 | 110 |

Jesus   Paul's letters   Post-New
                                                  Testament writings

*Time frame in which non-Pauline
books were written*

To summarize the evidence relating to the time frame, two statements can be made with confidence:

1. Paul's letters were written in the period c. 50-c. 65.
2. Apart from 2 John and Jude for which there are no sure references, the remaining parts of the New Testament were written after c. 33 and were in use by the nineties.

It is instructive to compare the literary evidence for Jesus with that of other famous men of antiquity. Roughly comparable is Tiberius, the emperor in whose time Jesus died. Born 42 B.C., Tiberius was emperor from A.D. 14 to 37. While Velleius Paterculus wrote in about A.D. 30 of Tiberius's earlier military exploits, our major sources are considerably later—Tacitus about A.D. 110, Suetonius about A.D. 120 and Dio Cassius about A.D. 220.

In Jesus' case there is a shorter time lapse between his life and the literature. Allowing c. A.D. 90 as the latest date possible for the Gospels, less than sixty years separate these books from their principal character. In the case of the Gospel of Mark, written by the year 70, a mere forty years separates Jesus from this text. At the end of the frame nearer Jesus we note that a mere seventeen years elapsed between Jesus and 1 Thessalonians.

A more extreme comparison might be made between Alexander the Great, who died in 323 B.C., and his major historian, Arrian, who wrote in A.D. 130s. The major outlines of Alexander's career are not doubted despite a period exceeding four hundred years separating the man and the chief source of information about him.

It is important to note three things about Jesus in the context of history writing in the ancient world. First, the time lapse between his life and the literature about it is short compared to that between the lives and the literature about other great figures of the times. Second, the number of authors contributing to the literature also compares very favorably with the number writing about other great figures. No less than nine or ten early authors, most of them writing independently of each other, refer to Jesus. Third, from the end of the epoch of the New Testament writings there was an unbroken and growing stream of Christian literature which establishes the existence of the literature of the New Testament by quoting from it. To this point we now turn.

FURTHER READING

F. F. Bruce, *The New Testament Documents: Are They Reliable?* 6th ed. (Downers Grove, Ill.: InterVarsity Press, 2003).

John A. T. Robinson, *Redating the New Testament* (Philadelphia: Westminster Press, 1976).

5

IS THE TRANSMISSION TRUSTWORTHY?

T he next logical question is, how do I know that what I now read in the New Testament is what was originally written? After all, nineteen hundred years have passed and the text could easily have been tampered with during that period. How trustworthy is the transmission?

AN UNUSUAL HABIT

"It was their habit on a fixed day to assemble," wrote Pliny, governor of Bithynia, informing Emperor Trajan about the meetings of the sect of the Christians. The assembling of Christians on a "fixed day" is taken for granted today. In the year A.D. 112 it was an oddity, something worth noting. At first they met in homes or in the open and, only after several centuries, in special Christian buildings. But wherever it was, meet they did—and on "a fixed day."

Forty or so years later, the Christian writer Justin described what happened in Rome when Christians assembled for their weekly meeting. This short extract shows how important the reading of the Scriptures was:

> On the day called Sunday all who live in cities or in the country gather together to the one place, and the memoirs of the apostles or the writings of the prophets are read, as long as time permits. (*First Apology* 67)

In Justin's day in Rome the "memoirs of the apostles," as he calls the Gospels, had been copied from earlier versions which went back less than a century to the Greek originals written by Matthew, Mark, Luke and John. We have no way of knowing how much hand copying stood between the "memoirs" mentioned by Justin and the originals, but it cannot have been many, given the slowness and expense of the copying process and the relatively brief space of time.[1]

Half a century after Justin, these Greek documents were translated into Latin for reading in Latin-speaking North Africa, Gaul and Spain, as well as Italy. The gospel spread quickly throughout the polyglot societies surrounding the Mediterranean. By the third and fourth centuries the New Testament was being translated into Coptic and Syriac. And so the process went on. In every country the gospel went to, in time local translations were made for the public reading of the Scriptures to the Christians assembled on a "fixed day" of the week.

This unusual "habit" of weekly meeting, which struck Pliny as worth noticing, continued uninterrupted through the centuries and remains a mark of Christianity. Sunday by Sunday, the public reading of the Scriptures has occurred from apostolic times until today.

PROFUSION OF MANUSCRIPTS

The "habit" of meeting, accompanied as it was by public Scripture reading, led to the proliferation and therefore the preservation of the Scriptures. In the early centuries the rapidly growing number of churches required an increased supply of copies. There still exist more than five thousand early manuscript copies of part or all of the New Testament in Greek. In addition, there are numerous early translations into Coptic, Latin, Syriac, Armenian, Georgian, etc. These are called the Versions. Let us not forget that Christianity spread in an unorganized, uncoordinated way. There can be no question of centralized publishing of these manuscripts.

So the expansion of the movement was matched by a profusion of manuscripts, many of which have survived through to modern times. There are more then five hundred manuscripts or manuscript fragments in Greek that have survived from the early centuries, evidence of the spread of Christianity in the Greek-speaking world.

One notable example is *Codex Sinaiticus*, a complete fourth-century edition of the New Testament that was discovered in 1844 at St. Catherine's monastery, Mt. Sinai. This codex owes its survival, like many other New Testament manuscripts, to a dry climate and the relative security of a Christian monastery and today is safely housed in the British Museum.

From much closer to the era of the New Testament we have a piece of papyrus known as p^{52} dating from the early second century containing part of John 18. From later in the second century we have one manuscript containing the Gospels and Acts (p^{45}) and another that has the letters of Paul (p^{46}). In other words, from the second century we have manuscripts that encompass the greater part of the New Testament. Additionally there are numerous surviving manuscripts in Latin, Syriac, Coptic and Armenian testifying to the rapid early rise of churches in the nations of the Mediterranean world.

This profusion of early manuscripts of the New Testament is in contrast with the few for Josephus's *Jewish War*. Josephus, a Pharisee and Jewish aristocrat, wrote his great history of the war of A.D. 66-70 between the Romans and Jews shortly after its cessation. It is a Greek work based on an Aramaic first draft and written very close in time to the Gospels. Apart from two collections of excerpts, there are only nine complete manuscripts in existence, the oldest of which is a fifth-century Latin translation. The remaining eight Greek manuscripts, of which only two are regarded as superior texts, are from the tenth century and later. If scholars are confident, as they are, of the integrity of Josephus's restored text, though based on so few and such late manuscripts, how much more might we be assured about the restored text of the Greek New Testament, based as it is on so many and such early manuscripts?

The contrast is even more dramatic with Tacitus's *Annals of Imperial Rome*, the chief historical source for the Roman world of New Testament times. There is only one surviving manuscript for *Annals* 1 to 6 (discovered c. 1510) and one for *Annals* 11 to 16 (discovered c. 1430). Neither manuscript is earlier than the Middle Ages. *Annals* 7 to 10 is missing.

Clearly it was that Christian "habit" of assembling on a "fixed day" to hear the Scriptures read that explains both the multiplicity and the survival of New Testament texts. During the Middle Ages these early manuscripts were kept secure by the monasteries. Today they are stored in modern libraries under carefully controlled conditions.

AN AVALANCHE OF EARLY CHRISTIAN BOOKS

While Christianity had small beginnings in the first half-century of its life, it rapidly expanded throughout the Greco-Roman world in the subsequent centuries. Only two centuries after the last book of the New Testament, Revelation, was written, the emperor Constantine virtually made Christianity the official religion of the Roman Empire. Throughout those two hundred years Christian intellectuals and leaders had been writing books defending and explaining the faith. Their collected writings comprise the ten large volumes of the *Ante-Nicene Fathers* library, each volume being several times longer than the whole New Testament.

These writers often quoted at length from the New Testament, and their quotations—called citations—are used as a check on the early manuscripts of the New Testament. It has been claimed that almost the whole New Testament could be recovered from the citations of those early Christian writers. Their books, like the New Testament manuscripts, were preserved through the Middle Ages by the monasteries.

When Josephus and Tacitus completed their manuscripts there was no immediate system for either preserving or copying what they had written. With the New Testament it was different. That collection of books became the much-copied Scriptures of a rapidly growing movement that soon became the state religion. Those Scriptures in turn gave rise to an immense output of early Christian literature that quoted them at great length and, in effect, preserved them. The growth of the monasteries in the fourth century coincided with the beginning of the Dark Ages. It was in the monasteries that the New Testament manuscripts, the writings of the early church, and the work of such writers as Josephus and Tacitus were preserved until the Renaissance, the invention of the printing press, and the development of modern museums and libraries.

How confident are modern scholars that the Greek text of the New Testament they translate is as it was originally written? Through the labors of textual critics who have collected and compared the manuscripts over the past two centuries, it can be stated that the major questions about the text have been resolved. For example, Mark 16:9-20 and John 8:1-11 are now believed not to have belonged to the original text of those Gospels, though

John 8:1-11 appears to be a genuine text from some other place in the Gospels. Apart from those two longer passages, what remain are numerous variant readings of individual words or short phrases. The footnotes of the Revised Standard Version of the Bible indicate the major variants, which occur at the rate of less than one per page. It is safe to say that substantial matters of Christian history or doctrine are not affected by whatever uncertainties remain. In reviewing the state of textual criticism Stephen Neill has commented that "we have a far better and more reliable text of the New Testament than of any other ancient work whatever, and the measure of uncertainty is really rather small."[2] Neill concluded:

> Anyone who reads the New Testament in any one of half a dozen recent Greek editions, or in any modern translation, can feel confident that, though there may be uncertainties in detail, in almost everything of importance he is close indeed to the text of the New Testament books as they were originally written.[3]

FURTHER READING

Bruce Manning Metzger, *A Textual Commentary on the Greek New Testament* (New York: United Bible Societies, 1975).

Stephen Neill, *The Interpretation of the New Testament, 1861-1961* (London: Oxford University Press, 1964).

Alexander Souter, *The Text and Canon of the New Testament* (London: Duckworth, 1960).

6

THE TWO WITNESSES

So far we have attempted to ask and answer the following questions: Did Jesus in fact live? Yes. The early non-Christian writers leave us with no doubt. Can we know the time frame in which the New Testament was written? Again, yes. In broad terms the literature came into existence within the period A.D. 33 to 95. Can we be confident about transmission of the manuscripts from those times to the present? Once more, yes. The sheer number of early texts guarantees that what we read is, for all practical purposes, what the original authors wrote.

The next logical question is, can we know that what we read of Jesus is a true account? Perhaps the story has been twisted somewhere in the period between Jesus' life and the time the literature about him was written. How confident are we that Matthew, Mark, Luke and John have told us the truth about Jesus and not given us some idealized, romantic version?

New Testament scholars have wrestled with this question for two centuries, and much work remains to be done. There are three matters, however, which have been resolved to the satisfaction of most of the experts:

1. Mark was written before Matthew and Luke.

2. Matthew and Luke broadly follow Mark's sequence and incorporate Markan material into their Gospels. Matthew, Mark and Luke are often called Synoptic Gospels, which means they are able to be arranged in parallel.[1]

3. John's outline of events does not easily dovetail with Mark's or vice versa.[2]

For the time being we will leave Matthew and Luke and concentrate on

Mark and John, whose presentations of the career of Jesus are so different. In Mark's account Jesus comes to Jerusalem only once—for the final week of his earthly life. By contrast, John often has Jesus in Jerusalem. In fact, sixteen of John's twenty-one chapters are set in Jerusalem. Clearly Mark and John are unsynoptic.

What makes the Gospels of Mark and John important is the concept of "witness". The writer of the Fourth Gospel makes direct claim to be a "witness" to Jesus (Jn 21:20, 24; cf. 19:35). In the other case there is early evidence that Mark wrote in collaboration with Peter, who often claims to be a "witness" to Jesus (Acts 2:32; 3:15; 5:32; 10:39-42; 1 Pet 5:1; 2 Pet 1:16-18). We defer for the moment discussion of the claims that the Gospels of John and Mark arise out of "witness." First we must ask, what is "witness"?

WITNESS IN THE NEW TESTAMENT

Christians today sometimes speak about "witnessing," by which they mean sharing their faith in an evangelistic way. In this context *witness* means telling about something that is personal, religious and subjective. But this is not the way *witness* is used in the New Testament.

The noun *witness* is used thirty-five times in the New Testament. Leaving aside the five references in the Book of Revelation where it is used in the sense of "martyr" the remaining thirty are used in the sense of "eyewitness." Here the dominant idea is of an onlooker who could "bear witness" in a court hearing for or against an accused person. The letter to the Hebrews comments that "a man who has violated the law of Moses dies without mercy at the testimony of two or three *witnesses*" (10:28, italics mine).

Any charge against an erring Christian (2 Cor 13:1; Mt 18:16) or local church leader (1 Tim 5:19) is, by the rule of the Old Testament (Deut 19:15), to be sustained by "two or three witnesses." At the trials of both Jesus (Mk 14:63) and Stephen (Acts 6:14; 7:58), evidence was given by "witnesses." These references indicate that a "witness" was someone who had been present at the time of an incident and who could give evidence of what he had seen or heard. It is the same idea when Paul calls "God to witness against" him (2 Cor 1:23; cf. Rom 1:9; Phil 1:8).

It is in this sense that the apostles were to be "witnesses" to Christ (Acts

1:8). The death of Judas left a gap to be filled to make up the number of twelve apostles (Acts 1:20). Peter stated the qualifications for the person to be chosen:

> One of the men who have accompanied us during all the time that the Lord Jesus went in and out among us, beginning from the baptism of John until the day when he was taken up from us—one of these men must become with us a *witness* to his resurrection. (Acts 1:21-22, italics mine)

Notice here two qualifications about the would-be apostle and "witness": he must have belonged to the physical company of those who were present with Jesus from the beginning of his public ministry until his ascension; and he must therefore be able to "witness" to the resurrection of Jesus as one who had been present at the time.

As the narrative of Acts unfolds, Peter repeatedly claims to have been a "witness" to (the death) and resurrection of Jesus:

> This Jesus God raised up, and of that we all are *witnesses*. (2:32)

> . . . the author of life, whom God raised from the dead. To this we are *witnesses*. (3:15)

> The God of our fathers raised Jesus. . . . And we are *witnesses* to these things. (5:30, 32)

> God raised him on the third day and made him manifest; not to all the people but to us who were chosen by God as *witnesses*. (10:40-41, italics mine)

Acting as a "witness" meant telling others what you had actually seen or heard with as much exactness as if giving evidence in a trial. In these references "witness" did not relate primarily to inward religious experience. "Witness" is about hard facts, about details of date, time, place and circumstances of empirical and observable events.

THE SERIOUSNESS OF FALSE WITNESS

Some of the Corinthians doubted there would be a resurrection of the dead

(1 Cor 15:12), doubtless referring the Greek idea of the immortality of the soul. In attempting to deal with this, Paul reminded them of the fundamentals of the apostolic gospel as received by him and handed over to them. The appropriate details to underline were that "he [Christ] was raised on the third day" (1 Cor 15:4) and "that he appeared to Cephas . . . to the twelve . . . to more than five hundred brothers and sisters . . . to James . . . to all the apostles. Last of all . . . also to me" (15:5-8 NRSV). By his words "whether then it was I or they, so we preach and so you believed" (15:11), Paul means simply "Jesus was seen by us risen from the dead; we the apostles told you about it and you believed."

Paul's logic is simple. If Christ has not been raised then all we have said about seeing him alive is empty, and, what is worse, we who have spoken have misrepresented God because we have "witnessed" that God did something that he did not in fact do. Paul and his fellow apostles and fellow witnesses will have been guilty of the ultimate blasphemy in lying about an important action of God. It was one thing in a court of law solemnly to give evidence as a "witness"; it was another to put God in the defendant's stand and to lie about his actions. In speaking as a "witness" to the resurrection of Jesus, nothing less than the truthfulness and integrity of God was at stake. It is as if Paul shudders at the implications.

The New Testament writers keep these things in clear focus. Either you were a "witness" or you were not. If Peter knew he was a "witness . . . of Christ" he also knew that the readers of his first letters had not seen Christ (1 Pet 5:1 and 1:8). On the other hand, Luke knew that he was not an eyewitness, while others before him were eyewitnesses of Christ (Lk 1:2). Similarly, the anonymous writer to the Hebrews declares himself to have heard not the Lord, but those who heard him (Heb 2:3). The disclaimers of Luke and the Hebrews writer make the claims of Peter all the more impressive. Only if you had seen and heard the Lord were you qualified to be a "witness."

This then is the background to the full meaning of "witness" and the claims made by John and for Mark. It is important, however, that we take careful note of what they write and why. John calls his work a "book" written so that the reader may "believe that Jesus is the Christ, the Son of God" (Jn 20:30-31). This suggests that John may be writing for those who already have some knowledge of Jesus to ensure that what they believe about him is correct. To this end the author has selected and written about a selection of the miracle signs of Jesus. He specifically claims not to have written comprehensively (Jn 20:30).

In his opening sentence, Mark refers to his document as a "gospel," which means "an important announcement of good news," either written or spoken. To look no further than Mark 1:14 we read of Jesus *speaking* the gospel. Unlike John, Mark does not tell us exactly why he is writing. We have to look for clues. While one purpose may be to give instruction and encouragement to believers (Mk 13:37) another may be to confront the non-Christian so that he will, like the centurion, declare Jesus to be "the Son of God" (Mk 15:39).

Thus our two documents are called by different titles and appear to have somewhat different objectives as well as different audiences. Mark is certainly written for Gentiles (see the author's explanation of Jewish customs in 7:3-4 and 14:12). The book of John appears to be written for Greek-speaking Jews (note the relative absence of explanations of things Jewish).

Stylistically, these two works differ both from each other and from a modern biography. A biographer today would be expected to describe the parents of the chief character's parents, the circumstances of his birth, as well as his education, appearance and upbringing—details Mark and John do not supply. It is important to read these texts on their terms, not on ours. While a historian may gather many facts about Jesus from John and Mark, it is extremely unlikely that he will then be able to write a biography in the modern manner. Each author has a message—a message about Jesus—that he expects readers to recognize and accept. Each Gospel is biographical but not a biography, historical but not a history. Biographies supply comprehensive information to inform the mind of the reader; Gospels inform the mind about Jesus in order to challenge the reader's will and behavior. It has been said that they read you as you read them. The Gospels address the whole person, not the intellect alone.

Did John and Mark know one another's writings? Scholars disagree about this, but it appears that our authors wrote independently of each other. Apart from their accounts of Good Friday and Easter Day, the only other narratives common to both are the baptism of John, the clearing of the temple, the feeding of the multitude, the anointing and the triumphal entry. The stories are told so differently that the possibility of literary dependence seems remote.

Further, how does one account for an innocent divergence such as the hour of the crucifixion? While both authors agree that the crucifixion occurred on the day before the Sabbath (Jn 19:31; Mk 15:42), in Mark Jesus is crucified at "the third hour" (9 a.m.; see 15:25) while in John the trial before Pilate is still in progress at "the sixth hour" (noon; see 19:14). While for some this difference is unpalatable, it may, in fact, enhance the deeper historicity of the account. Perfect agreement in every detail might justifiably arouse a suspicion of some kind of collusion between the authors. As they stand, the two versions, with their distinctive styles and various loose ends, encourage confidence that our writers are men of truth writing independently of each other, and that through them we, the readers, are in contact with the events as they occurred.

The Old Testament called for not one but two or three witnesses (see Deut 19:15). In the Gospels of John and Mark we have two independent, written "witnesses" to Jesus. Through their "witness" we, the readers, are able to arrive at a verdict, based on evidence, about Jesus of Nazareth.

FURTHER READING

Robert A. Guelich, "Mark, Gospel of," in *Dictionary of Jesus and the Gospels,* ed. J. B. Green, S. McKnight and I. H. Marshall (Downers Grove, Ill.: InterVarsity Press, 1992), pp. 512-25.

Leon L. Morris, *This Is the Testimony* (Melbourne, Australia: Baker Memorial Lecture, Ridley College, 1970).

Marianne Meye Thompson, "John, Gospel of," in *Dictionary of Jesus and the Gospels,* ed. J. B. Green, S. McKnight and I. H. Marshall (Downers Grove, Ill.: InterVarsity Press, 1992), pp. 368-83.

H. E. W. Turner, *Jesus, Master and Lord* (Geneva, Ala.: A. R. Allenson, 1954).

7

WITNESS ONE

The Disciple Whom Jesus Loved

The author of the Fourth Gospel makes the direct claim that he was a witness of Jesus. In his account of the crucifixion he describes how the soldiers broke the legs of the other victims before discovering that Jesus was already dead, whereupon a soldier "pierced his side with a spear." The writer then adds, "He who saw it has borne witness—his testimony is true, and he knows that he tells the truth—that you also may believe" (Jn 19:35).

The context makes it clear that the only disciple near the scene of the crucifixion was "the disciple whom [Jesus] loved" (Jn 19:26). He saw what happened and bore witness about it. Further, he assures his readers that his testimony is true and may be believed.

The final episode in this Gospel is a dialogue between Jesus and Peter, in which Peter enquires what is to happen to "the disciple whom Jesus loved" who was following them (21:20-21). The author continues, "This is the disciple who is bearing witness to these things, and who has written these things; and we know that his testimony is true" (21:24).

This is *written* witness by the "disciple whom Jesus loved," who was present with Jesus and Peter by the Sea of Tiberias when, for the third time since his crucifixion, Jesus manifested himself alive to his disciples (Jn 21:14). The writer of this book intends us to understand that he is the "disciple whom Jesus loved."

Who, then, are those referred to as "we," who know that the testimony of the beloved disciple is true? It is sometimes suggested that these persons are in fact responsible for writing the Fourth Gospel. The text, however, clearly states "this is the disciple . . . who has written these things," referring to the disciple whom Jesus loved. Those who are described as "we" authenticate what is written, but they are not the authors. So who are they?

The clue to their identity is found at the beginning of John's book—"we have beheld his glory" (1:14). When he subsequently states, "Jesus . . . manifested his glory; and his disciples believed in him" (Jn 2:11), it is clear, since "glory" is present in both passages, "his disciples" in chapter 2 are the "we" of chapter 1. "We" represents the disciples who accompanied Jesus and who witnessed his signs (see Jn 20:30).

This book, however, implies that the group continued and that it was only after Jesus left them that many of the things he said and did were understood. After the temple-clearing incident the author comments:

> When . . . he was raised from the dead, his disciples *remembered* that he had said this; and they believed the scripture and the word which Jesus had spoken. (Jn 2:22, italics mine)

Similarly, he observes after the entry to Jerusalem:

> His disciples did not *understand* this at first; but when Jesus was glorified, then they remembered that this had been written of him and had been done to him. (Jn 12:16, italics mine)

By writing in this vein the author means for us to understand that it was the disciples' experience of the Holy Spirit after the glorification of Jesus (Jn 7:39) that enabled them to "remember" (see Jn 14:26) and to "understand" (see Jn 16:13-15) what Jesus had said and done while he was with them. Moreover, in the absence of Jesus, this group would need to be kept true to his word in what would be, for them, a situation of conflict and hostility (Jn 16:1-4; 17:11-17).

In summary, the "we" of John 21:24, who know that the testimony of the beloved disciple is true, are those disciples who were with Jesus. They witnessed his signs and saw his glory, and, since Jesus' glorification, have entered into a deeper understanding of Jesus through the activity of the Holy Spirit in the context of opposition and suffering. The beloved disciple speaks as one of them; they confirm the truth of what he says. Significantly, there is the same interplay between individual and group in the first letter of John. On the one hand it states "*we* are writing this" (1 Jn 1:4) while on the other "I am writing this" (1 Jn 2:1). Our conclusion is that both the Gospel and first letter of John were written by an individual who was a member of a close-knit group that he represented and for which he spoke.

WHO IS THE DISCIPLE WHOM JESUS LOVED?

The author of the book, "the disciple whom Jesus loved," does not directly disclose his identity. Evidently he was so well known in his circle that he did not need to give his name. Nevertheless, there are three clues in the text that assist us to identify him.

First, he was an intimate friend of Jesus. He was "one of his disciples" who was "lying close to the breast of Jesus" with Peter nearby, perhaps on the other side next to Jesus (Jn 13:23-24). This disciple also stood with Mary, the mother of Jesus, near the cross. Such was the confidence of Jesus in the man that he was henceforth to enjoy a son-mother relationship with Mary in his own home (Jn 19:26-27).

Second, he was a close colleague of Peter. This disciple accompanied Peter on Easter morning to check the story of Mary Magdalene that the stone had been removed from the entrance to the tomb (Jn 20:2). The discussion by the Sea of Tiberias indicates that he was a close friend both of Jesus and Simon Peter (Jn 21:20-21).

Third, the "disciple whom Jesus loved" was one of the group of seven disciples by the Sea of Tiberias comprising Simon Peter, Thomas called the Twin, Nathanael of Cana in Galilee, the sons of Zebedee and two others of his disciples (Jn 21:2).

Since "the disciple whom Jesus loved" was an intimate friend of Jesus and a close colleague of Peter, the most likely candidate is one of "the sons of Zebedee." Because James Zebedee was martyred c. A.D. 43 (Acts 12:2), the logical conclusion has been to identify this anonymous disciple with John Zebedee. The probability is strengthened by complete absence of any reference to the name "John" in this Gospel, except for John the Baptist. Similarly the word *Zebedee* occurs in this book only in the passage quoted.

The earliest list of the New Testament books, the Muratorian Fragment, dated c. 180-200, states: "The fourth book of the gospel is that of John, one of the disciples." Irenaeus, who was a second-century writer and a pupil of Polycarp, who learned from John Zebedee, wrote: "Lastly John, the disciple of the Lord, who had leant back on his breast, once more set forth the gospel, while residing at Ephesus in Asia."[1]

The opinion of second-century Christian authors is that "the disciple whom Jesus loved" was John Zebedee and he wrote the Fourth Gospel. As we shall see, however, many modern scholars do not agree.

WHAT KIND OF BOOK?

What kind of document is it that John has written and why did he write it? Since this is the Scripture that many modern evangelists say should be read first, we assume that it is evangelistic in character. But is it? What does the author himself say?

> Now Jesus did many other signs in the presence of the disciples, which are not written in this book; but these are written that you may believe that Jesus is the Christ, the Son of God, and that believing you may have life in his name. (Jn 20:30-31)

The words translated here as "you may believe" do not have the meaning "come to believe" in the original but "go on believing."[2] What John has written, therefore, is not primarily an evangelistic tract designed for people to come to believe *in* Jesus. (He never refers to what he has written as a "gospel.") It is a "book" written to assist Christian readers to continue believing that Jesus is the Messiah, the Son of God.

The author does not need to tell the basic gospel story again; his readers, apparently, already know it. Their need was for a clearer and stronger understanding of who Jesus was. In order to help them, the writer, having considered the many miracle signs of Jesus, chose seven to demonstrate the true identity of Jesus. These miracle signs are

- the turning of water to wine at Cana (2:1-11)
- the healing of the son of the nobleman in Capernaum (4:46-54)
- the healing of the cripple at the pool in Jerusalem (5:1-9)

- the feeding of the multitude in the wilderness (6:1-15)
- the healing of the blind man in Jerusalem (9:1-8)
- the raising of Lazarus from the dead in Bethany (11:1-44)
- the resurrection of Jesus himself in Jerusalem (20:1-29)

Why did John select these miracles rather than others?

One reason may be that they are so unambiguously miraculous. As we reflect on these seven incidents, there is simply no other interpretation possible. In each case, a great miracle has occurred. Just under *180 gallons* of water were made into wine; the boy was healed *from a distance;* the man had been crippled for *thirty-eight years; five thousand* men were fed; the man was *born blind;* Lazarus had been buried for *four days* and Jesus for *three days.* Such incidents could not be ascribed to imagination or psychic power!

A further reason is that several of the miracles appear to have been selected to help the readers decide to give up their allegiance to Judaism and to commit all to Jesus. The water that Jesus made into wine had been used for "Jewish rites of purification" (Jn 2:6). The miracle of the loaves and fish provided an opportunity for Jesus to describe himself as the "true bread" (Jn 6:32-33), as compared with the "manna in the wilderness" (Jn 6:31). These "signs" demonstrate that Jesus fulfills and ends the old covenant, so that further involvement in Judaism as a religious system is now pointless.

The author, therefore, is using these miracles and what Jesus says about them to persuade the readers of the rightness of what he is saying. He is not writing a history or a biography of Jesus but is attempting to strengthen in his readers a particular view of Jesus. The question for us is, does he use *historical* information in arguing that case? The answer is that the data contained in this book is historical and geographical in character and that, of the four Evangelists, this writer gives us more specifically historical and topographical information than the other three combined. Let us consider three kinds of historical data in the Fourth Gospel.

1. Buildings and landscape. The author refers many times to buildings and places in Palestine. As these have been progressively subjected to investigation, there has emerged a healthy respect for the author's knowledge and accuracy of these matters. Let us look at four examples.

Jacob's well. There is a very deep well—approximately 130 feet deep—a few hundred yards from the traditional site of Joseph's tomb from which Mount Gerizim, the sacred mountain of the Samaritans, can be seen. A little over half a mile to the north of the well is a village called Askar, which was apparently known as Sychar in the fourth century.[3] Also, the Talmud twice refers to a spring called Ain Soker, which may be identical with the fountain in the well near Askar. Clearly the Talmud's "Soker" resembles John's "Sychar." The writer of John 4, apparently, was familiar with this well:

> He had to pass through Samaria. So he came to a city of Samaria called Sychar, near the field that Jacob gave to his son Joseph. Jacob's well was there. . . . The [Samaritan] woman said to him, . . . "The well is deep. . . . Our fathers worshiped on this mountain." (Jn 4:4, 11, 20)

Going down to Capernaum. The threefold reference to "down" is an easy detail to miss, buried as it is within the narrative of John 4. The Cana of John's Gospel has been identified with Khirbet Qana, which is approximately nine miles from Nazareth. It is significant that between Cana, where Jesus talked to the official, and Capernaum, where the official's son was, the land falls from well above sea level to about 650 feet below sea level, a drop of many hundred yards. The writer has shown, in this narrative, an accurate understanding of the topography of western Galilee.

> So he came again to Cana in Galilee. . . . And at Capernaum there was an official whose son was ill. . . . He went and begged him to *come down* and heal his son. . . . "Sir, *come down* before my child dies." . . . As he *was going down,* his servants met him. (Jn 4:46-47, 49, 51, italics mine)

The pool of Bethzatha. Archaeologists have uncovered a double pool surrounded by four porticoes, with a fifth on a rock gangway between the two pools. The pool was approximately fifty feet deep, making it necessary for a crippled person not only to be assisted to the water but also supported in it. This is most likely the site described by John.

> Now there is in Jerusalem by the Sheep Gate a pool, in Hebrew called Bethzatha, which has five porticoes. (Jn 5:2)

The temple in winter. Here is a piece of incidental information upon which nothing in the narrative depends. The Maccabean Feast of Dedication (Hanukkah) occurs in winter, just as Christmas in Australia occurs in midsummer. Jesus seeks shelter from the weather in a particular place, Solomon's porch, which is part of the temple of Herod. If someone wrote of a person seeking shelter from the sun on Christmas day in the Bennelong Restaurant in the Sydney Opera House, it would be reasonable to conclude that he had firsthand knowledge of the Australian climate and of a Sydney landmark in the period after the year 1973 when the Opera House was completed. We conclude that the author of this Gospel had firsthand understanding of the climate of Judea and of the architecture of the temple in the period before A.D. 70 when it was destroyed.

> It was the feast of the Dedication at Jerusalem; it was winter, and Jesus was walking in the temple, in the portico of Solomon. (Jn 10:22-23)

Finally we may note that the fourth Evangelist mentions as many as twelve places not referred to in the other Gospels. In this regard two experts in the archaeology of Palestine have noted:

> It is . . . the single most intensely "theological" or "symbolic" treatise of the New Testament, namely the gospel of John, which is peppered with side references to the geography of Palestine.

Some of these places—"this mountain" [Gerizim] (Jn 4:20), the pool of Siloam (9:7) and the Kidron valley (18:1)—can be located precisely. Even if all do not have certain identification there is, nevertheless, an air of authenticity in the author's manner of description. He wrote of "Bethany beyond the Jordan" (1:28); "Cana in Galilee" (2:1; 4:46)—thereby distinguishing it from "Cana in Sidon"; "Aenon near Salim" and the fact that there was "much water there" (3:23); Ephraim, a town "near the wilderness" (11:54); "a place called The Pavement, and in Hebrew, Gabbatha" (19:13). The qualifying phrases accompanying these place names strengthen the impression that they are precise geographical locations.[4]

It is this author who records Nathanael's question, "Can anything good come out of Nazareth?" (Jn 1:46), which to most readers is fairly meaning-

less. Similarly, near the end of the Gospel, it seems of little account to read
that Nathanael is from Cana (Jn 21:2). What archaeologists have discovered,
however, is that the village they have identified as Cana is quite close to Nazareth. It looks as though Nathanael's sarcastic question is a local proverb
about a nearby village that, it now transpires, was very small and off the
beaten track. The archaeological evidence is that the author had minute local
knowledge, which he discloses in quite inconspicuous ways.

The Evangelist knows that it is two days' journey from Bethany beyond
Jordan (Jn 1:28, 35, 43; 2:1) to Cana, one day from Cana to Capernaum
(4:52) and two days from Bethany beyond Jordan to Bethany near Jerusalem
(10:40—11:18).[5]

It is difficult to escape the conclusion that the fourth Evangelist was quite
familiar with the topography and buildings of southern Palestine. Noted archaeologists Eric Meyers and James Strange comment:

> These examples could be multiplied many times and supplemented
> with examples of lore, customs and other bits of information known to
> the author of this Gospel. The point we wish to make, however, is sim-
> ply that an unprejudiced reading of the Gospel of John seems to sug-
> gest that it is in fact based on a historical and geographical tradition,
> though not one that simply repeats information from the synoptics.[6]

2. Consistency with the historical context. The Jewish historian Josephus referred to the war between the Jews and Romans in A.D. 66-70 in Palestine as

> the greatest not only of the wars of our own time, but, so far as ac-
> counts have reached us, well nigh of all that ever broke out between
> cities or nations. (*The Jewish War* 1.1)

This war separated the history before it from subsequent history in the
way a massive freeway cuts a swath through the countryside and separates
one side absolutely from the other. Tens of thousands of Jews were killed.
Hundreds of villages were destroyed and many parts of the landscape de-
nuded as trees were cut down for the Roman siegeworks. Above all, the temple was destroyed and with it many parts of Jerusalem. All the associated

systems—the rosters of priests, the provision of sacrificial animals—were no more. Gone were the chief priests and the administrative infrastructure provided by the Sanhedrin. Judea came under a more direct Roman military rule. The Sadducean party disappeared and also various rebel factions like the Zealots and the Sicarii. The more extreme Pharisaic party, the Shammaites, passed out of existence, leaving only the benign Hillelites.

Life was as radically different for the Jews after that war in Judea as it was for the Russians after the 1917 revolution, when Lenin and the Communists replaced the regime of the czars. The point is that the fourth Evangelist not only does not hint that such a catastrophic war had occurred, but his story is told in terms of what life was like before, not after, that war. Quite innocently in the narrative certain Jews comment that it has "taken forty-six years to build this temple" (Jn 2:20). In another place the writer comments, "Now there is in Jerusalem by the Sheep Gate a pool . . . which has five porticoes" (Jn 5:2). It is natural to infer from the present tense of the verb *is* that both buildings were still standing at the time of writing.

C. H. Dodd was struck by the trial narrative in the Gospel of John and the relationship reflected there between the Roman governor and the high priestly leaders:

> It is pervaded with a lively sense for the situation as it was in the last half-century before the extinction of Judaean local autonomy. It is aware of the delicate relations between the native and imperial authorities. . . . These conditions were present in Judaea before A.D. 70, and not later and not elsewhere.[7]

While Dodd regards the final writer of the Gospel as well removed in time and place from his excellent pre-70 sources, John A. T. Robinson regards it as much more likely that the primitive source and the final writer is one and the same person.[8] It is surely more logical to believe that the Gospel was written in the period which it purports to describe, that is, before 66. After A.D. 70, life in Palestine was so different that it would not be possible for someone unfamiliar with the earlier period to have described accurately from his imagination Jesus at the Feast of Dedication (wintertime) walking in Solomon's portico in the temple at Jerusalem.

3. People. The fourth Evangelist also shows that his presentation is rooted in history by the references he makes to people. It is interesting that the information conveyed by this writer has not been derived from the other Gospels. Yet there is no reason to doubt the authenticity of this information. Let us consider six people.

John the Baptist. The fourth Evangelist alone specifies the places where John the Baptist baptized: "Bethany beyond the Jordan" (Jn 1:28) and "Aenon near Salim" (Jn 3:23). Only this writer informs us that John the Baptist had "disciples" (Jn 1:35; 3:25) and that two of these subsequently formed the nucleus of Jesus' disciples (Jn 1:35-42). This Evangelist alone tells us that Jesus and John, with their respective groups of followers, operated in parallel for some time before John was imprisoned (Jn 3:22-24), and that the disciples of Jesus baptized people into their group—more, in fact, than John the Baptist did into his group (Jn 3:22; 4:1-2). If we possessed only the Synoptic Gospels we would assume that Jesus' public ministry began when John's was finished (Mk 1:14 and parallels). The Fourth Gospel shows us that, for a period at least, the two ministries overlapped. The statement "John did no sign" (Jn 10:41), found only in this Gospel, is consistent with other evidence about John the Baptist. As a historical source for John the Baptist, we conclude that this Gospel contains more detailed information than the Synoptic Gospels.

Nathanael. Nathanael is mentioned only by the Evangelist John, though it is possible that he is, in fact, Nathanael bar Tholomew (Son of Tholomew).[9] He was from Cana in Galilee (Jn 21:2) and was known to Philip of Bethsaida, which was also the home town of Andrew and Peter (Jn 1:44-45). Though skeptical of any good thing, especially the Messiah, coming from nearby Nazareth, he subsequently acknowledged Jesus as "King of Israel" (Jn 1:46-49). Nathanael was one of seven persons to whom the risen Jesus revealed himself in Galilee (Jn 21:1-2). Everything John tells us of this man— his town of origin, his association with other Galileans, his sarcastic proverb about Nazareth—suggests authentic historical information.

Joseph. In the Synoptic Gospels Joseph is mentioned only at the time of the conception and birth of Jesus, that is, in about 7 B.C. From these sources it would be easy to conclude that Joseph had died some time after the birth of his other children (Mk 6:3) and the commencement of Jesus' public ministry c. A.D. 29. The Gospel of John, however, makes it clear that Joseph was alive at the time Jesus fed the multitudes in the wilderness (6:42).[10] Had John depended on the Synoptics for his information, it is unlikely Joseph would have been mentioned at all.

In both of John's references Jesus is spoken of as "the son of Joseph" (Jn 1:45; 6:42), which is the way Jesus' Galilean contemporaries would have referred to him. Later, however, Jesus was said to have been "born of a woman," a statement that both believers and opponents used, though for different reasons. Paul, the believer, meant to imply that the conception of Jesus was by an act of God, without sexual intercourse, whereas in the Talmud Jesus was a bastard born out of wedlock from union between a Roman soldier Pandira ("Panther") and Mary (*b. Shabbat* 104b). John's reference to Jesus as "son of Joseph" may be a very early Galilean tradition. Again, the evidence from John, in this case relating to Jesus "son of Joseph," who was alive during the public ministry of Jesus, has all the marks of authenticity and historicity.

Nicodemus. Nicodemus, who is referred to only by this Evangelist, appears three times within the narrative. On the first occasion, in Jerusalem (Jn 3:1-15), he acknowledges that Jesus is a miracle worker and teacher. In the course of the narrative it emerges that Nicodemus is a member of the sect of the Pharisees (3:1) and indeed a leading rabbi (3:10) and further, that he was a "ruler of the Jews" (3:1) or member of the Jewish senate, the Sanhedrin.

On the second occasion, also in Jerusalem (Jn 7:50) he speaks as "one of them," that is, as belonging to the "authorities" and "Pharisees" (7:48), thus confirming what is stated in the first passage.

On the third occasion, again in Jerusalem (Jn 19:38-39), Nicodemus appears with Joseph of Arimathea to collect the body of Jesus. The quantity, one hundred pounds of mixed myrrh and aloes brought by Nicodemus to apply to the body, is generous but not outlandish. The implication is that this Pharisaic rabbi and Sanhedrin member was also wealthy.

John's information about Nicodemus is detailed, consistent and soberly related without any trace of romanticism. There is no reason to doubt the authenticity of Nicodemus.

Caiaphas. Caiaphas is mentioned twice by Matthew, once by Luke, once in

Acts, five times by John and not at all by Mark. From Matthew we learn that
Caiaphas was high priest of the temple and president of the Sanhedrin (Mt
26:3, 57) at the time of the crucifixion, which is in line with Josephus's chronology (*Antiquities* 18.35, 95; cf. 18.64). Luke, however, refers to the "high
priesthood" of Annas and Caiaphas (Lk 3:2; cf. Acts 4:6). This is curious, since
Annas's high priesthood ended in A.D. 15 (*Antiquities* 18.27). Of the various
sources of information about Caiaphas, John alone tells us that he was the son-
in-law of Annas (Jn 18:13), which may explain why Luke linked the two
names as does John (Jn 18:13, 24). Twice John states that "Caiaphas . . . was
high priest that year" (Jn 11:49; 18:13), indicating, perhaps, that Annas re-
tained the real power even after he was deposed, possibly delegating it from
time to time to his son-in-law. Whatever the precise arrangements, it is from
John once again that the distinctive information emerges.

Caiaphas's name appears on an ossuary (his bone coffin) discovered in
Jerusalem in 1990.

Pilate. Pontius Pilate, Roman prefect of Judea (A.D. 26-36), is referred to
extensively in the New Testament, as he is also in the writings of Josephus
and Philo. The latter sources, particularly Philo, depict Pilate as ruthless and
unscrupulous. Some scholars, therefore, have expressed incredulity at the
relative weakness of character of Pilate portrayed in the Synoptic accounts
(see especially Lk 23:18-25).

It is the fourth Evangelist who supplies information that helps explain
why Pilate behaved in such an unusual way in his trial of Jesus. It is found
in the words of the Jews to Pilate: "If you release this man, you are not Caesar's friend; every one who makes himself a king sets himself against Caesar"
(Jn 19:12). Pilate owed his appointment as governor of Judea not to his aristocratic birth but to his "friendship" with the emperor Tiberius. This "friendship" would have been established in terms of contemporary patronage con-
vention by the emperor's deliberate kindness or favor toward Pilate.
Absolute loyalty would have been expected in return. The release of a self-
proclaimed king in a Roman province would have been a clear act of disloy-
alty to one's "friend," the emperor. Thus John alone conveys that it was not
Pilate's weakness but the Jews' blackmail that accounted for the governor's
uncharacteristic behavior.[11]

Is the Fourth Gospel historical in character? The wealth of information relating to places, to the specific context of the pre-A.D. 70 period and to the details about named individuals require our acknowledgment that this piece of literature is genuinely historical.

TWO PROBLEMS

Few New Testament scholars take account of what is, in my opinion, the clear historical character of the Fourth Gospel. For many, the historical question is settled in the negative, without further investigation, because of two problems associated with this Gospel. These two problems are seen to be so troublesome that scant attention is paid to the substantial historical element in the book.

A secondary source? The first problem is well stated by Günther Bornkamm:

> The Gospel according to John has so different a character in comparison with the other three, and is to such a degree the product of a developed theological reflection, that we can only treat it as a secondary source.[12]

It is agreed that this author's Gospel is "the product of a developed theological reflection." The book is marked with powerful symbolism, as in the words "it was night" (Jn 13:30), the writer's comment on Judas going out to betray Jesus. His love of imagery may be seen also in the repeated use of the "glory" motif associated with the death and resurrection of Jesus (for example, Jn 12:23; cf. 7:39). This is different from the Synoptic accounts, where glory is associated with the second coming and where the transfiguration, in effect, is a preview of his coming splendor. To focus our attention on the glorification of Jesus in his crucifixion and resurrection, John daringly omits the transfiguration episode.

It does not follow, however, that such symbolism makes John a "secondary" source. There are three reasons why the Fourth Gospel should not be regarded as secondary.

First, comparison with the few stories common to the Synoptics and John indicates that John is not derived from, but is independent of, other sources.

Consider, for example, the clearing of the temple in the accounts of Mark and John:

Mark 11:15-17

[15]And he entered the temple and began to drive out those who sold and those who bought in the temple, and he overturned the tables of the money-changers and the seats of those who sold pigeons; [16]and he would not allow any one to carry anything through the temple. [17]And he taught, and said to them, "Is it not written, 'My house shall be called a house of prayer for all the nations'? But you have made it a den of robbers."

John 2:14-16

[14]In the temple he found those who were selling oxen and sheep and pigeons, and the money-changers at their business. [15]And making a whip of cords, he drove them all, with the sheep and oxen, out of the temple; and he poured out the coins of the money-changers and overturned their tables. [16]And he told those who sold the pigeons, "Take these things away; You shall not make my Father's house a house of trade."

The basic story is common to both accounts so that there is little doubt that both are recounting the same incident. Yet there are numerous differences that make it unlikely that John has copied from Mark's text. For example, John leaves out "those who bought," Jesus overturning "the seats of those who sold pigeons" and the fact that he "would not allow any one to carry anything through the temple." On the other hand, John includes details such as "sheep and oxen," "making a whip of cords" and "he poured out the coins of the money-changers." Add to these omissions and inclusions the different comment made by Jesus in each account, and it appears highly unlikely that either of these accounts has been derived from the other.

The position of this incident in the Fourth and the Synoptic Gospels is a puzzle. Unless Jesus cleared the temple on two different occasions, which is not impossible, we have the problem that the Synoptics put it at the end and John puts it at the beginning. It may be that this Gospel is more thematic than chronological at some points, in which case we can accept that it is John who has relocated the incident. Nevertheless, it should be noted that it is, as we have suggested, an independent source, with more explicit information than Mark, and therefore in no sense a secondary source.

Second, the evidence relating to buildings and places, historical context and specific people shows that this writer was consciously utilizing historical information. There are many more pieces of specific information in the Fourth Gospel than in the other Gospels. This document is a primary, not a derived or secondary, document.

Third, comparison with parallel passages in the early-second-century writer Ignatius, bishop of Antioch, shows that John was not the very late author many believe him to be. Compare, for example:

Ignatius	John
For it [the Spirit] knoweth whence it cometh and whither it goeth. (*Philadelphians* 7.1)	The wind blows where it wills . . . but you do not know whence it comes or whither it goes. (Jn 3:8)

Passages such as this indicate that Ignatius knew and used the Fourth Gospel. Since Ignatius wrote early in the second century, it follows that this Gospel was written during the first century and therefore is not demonstrably later than the other Gospels.

These three pieces of evidence—the independence from Mark, the many historical details found only in John and origin of John's Gospel prior to Ignatius—make it clear that it is not a secondary source. Rather it is as primary a historical source as any other within the New Testament.

The presupposition underlying Bornkamm's statement is that a "developed" theology means a theology written later than less developed ones. But one has only to read the early-second-century Christian literature, such as *1 Clement* or the *Letter of Polycarp,* to discover that although written later than the Gospel of Mark or Paul's letter to the Galatians, the later theology is in these cases less theologically developed. While it is agreed that the theology of the Fourth Gospel is "developed," it does not follow that it is in any way diminished historically. It is preferable to regard this Gospel as the most developed theologically, and at the same time, the most explicitly historical of the four Gospels.

The speeches of Jesus in John. The second problem relates to the expansive style of speech used by Jesus in John's Gospel compared with pithy comparisons and parables in the Synoptics. It is argued that if Jesus spoke in one style in Matthew, the speaker in John cannot have been Jesus, and that the Evangelist must have composed the speeches of Jesus. The force of this argument must be recognized, since the style and vocabulary used throughout the Fourth Gospel are uniform and it is sometimes difficult to say where the words of Jesus end and those of the Evangelist commence. This is a real problem; nevertheless, two comments may be made.

First, the setting of the teachings of Jesus in the Fourth Gospel is different from the Synoptic tradition. In the Synoptic Gospels it is the Galilean ministry to country folk that is emphasized, whereas in John, Jesus is mostly in Jerusalem either debating with professional rabbis or speaking in private to the disciples. Jesus obviously possessed excellent communication skills, so we should not be surprised that he used different styles of speech in different situations. He addressed large crowds in the open but he also spoke privately to individuals indoors. He employed the conventions of the day in preaching on the set text in the synagogue, and he engaged in verbal sparring in debates with the scribes.[13]

In the Gospels we observe Jesus speaking prophetically and proverbially, polemically and pastorally. If a modern politician is able to alter his style from the party room to Congress to the public platform to radio talkback, how much more variation in style might we expect from a skillful communicator like Jesus?

Second, in John's Gospel Jesus says things differently; but he does not teach different things. In the Synoptics, for example, Jesus clearly taught that God was to be related to as "Father." The difference is that there are only twenty such references in all the Synoptic sources combined, and more than one hundred in John. In John's Gospel Jesus teaches on fewer subjects but with greater deliberation and repetition; the difference is in the style and not the content.

JOHN ZEBEDEE

Implicit in the doubts surrounding the Fourth Gospel is the unlikelihood that a Galilean fisherman could have written this profound book. Reference is made to the book of Acts, where Peter and John are said to be "uneducated, common men" (4:13). How could such men write our Gospels? Note, however, that this is the perception of the rulers, elders, scribes and chief priests (Acts 4:5-6) who, as professors and judges, were members of an intellectual and religious elite. The words translated "uneducated" and "common" (Greek: *agrammatos* and *idiōtēs*) do not mean Peter and John were illiterate, but compared with those who made the observation, they were nonprofessionals and laymen.

John Zebedee was from a socioeconomic class that used hired servants (Mk 1:20), so his circumstances may well have been comparable with the family of the prodigal son, which also had hired servants (Lk 15:17, 22, 26). John himself was not an employed hand but the member of a partnership of fishermen (Lk 5:10). His mother, Salome (Mk 15:40 = Mt 27:56), was one of a group of women who "ministered to [Jesus]" (Mk 15:41), which means that they "provided materially" for him. Salome was probably included in Luke's description of the "many" women who "provided for" Jesus and the Twelve "out of their means" (Lk 8:3). The mention of Joanna, wife of Chuza, Herod's steward, among these women, may indicate that the Zebedee family was at least middle class. Further, it is likely that the unnamed disciple who was "known to the high priest" (Jn 18:15-16) was, in fact, John Zebedee. Reference to him as "another disciple" (Jn 18:15) and "the other disciple" (Jn 18:16) certainly resembles "the other disciple, the one whom Jesus loved" (Jn 20:2). Peter is present with this "other disciple" in both passages, strengthening the likelihood that it is John. Acquaintance with the high priest would imply that this disciple belonged to the middle or upper strata of Jewish society.

By New Testament times, Palestine was Hellenized to a significant degree, with perhaps a majority of middle-class persons able to speak both Aramaic and Greek. Based as he was at busy Capernaum in "Galilee of the Gentiles" and belonging to the socioeconomic group described, it is reasonable to expect that John Zebedee is bilingual, with Greek as his second language. John A. T. Robinson commented that the fourth Evangelist was a writer "whose first language was evidently Aramaic and who wrote correct, though limited, Greek."[14]

John Zebedee the disciple of Jesus, along with his brother James and Peter, was one of the inner trio. He was one of the first called into Jesus' company (Mk 1:19). In addition to his experience as a member of the Twelve, he was a privileged witness to

- the healing of Peter's mother-in-law (Mk 1:29)
- the raising of the daughter of Jairus (Mk 5:37)
- the transfiguration (Mk 9:2)
- the Olivet discourse (Mk 13:3)
- the testing in Gethsemane (Mk 14:33)

If ever a person was singularly well equipped by experience to write a Gospel, it was John Zebedee.

This was not the end. Though younger than his brother James (Mk 1:19), John is given precedence over James after the resurrection (Acts 1:13). It is only John who is regularly mentioned with Peter in the earliest history of Christianity, both in Jerusalem (Acts 3—4) and also in Samaria (Acts 8:14-25). Along with James, brother of Jesus, and Peter, John is mentioned as one of the three "pillars" of the Jerusalem church who took part in the far-reaching missionary agreement in Jerusalem c. 47 (Gal 2:7-9). In addition to his three years in the fellowship of Jesus, John Zebedee was to act as a leader of the Jerusalem church for approximately fifteen years:

A.D. 30-33: Disciple of Jesus

A.D. 33-47: "Pillar" apostle of Jerusalem church

Then, so far as the New Testament is concerned, John Zebedee disappears from view. But there can be little doubt that he had the education and the experience to write the Gospel that bears his name.

TWO OPTIONS: TRUE OR FALSE

Two connected views about the Fourth Gospel are expressed by a number of New Testament scholars. On the one hand they reject its authorship by an original disciple while, on the other, they praise literary and theological qualities of his book. Raymond E. Brown refers to the author as a "master preacher and theologian" who was nevertheless "not famous."[15] C. K. Barrett states that "the evangelist" was "perhaps the greatest theologian in all the history of the church" but "was now forgotten. His name was unknown."[16]

The evidence from the second century is quite the reverse. The author was indeed "famous"; he was John Zebedee. Why is it that some modern scholars balk at the testimony of Irenaeus, whose teacher Polycarp was a pupil of John Zebedee? Why will they not accept the considerable weight of internal evidence which identifies "the disciple whom Jesus loved" with John Zebedee? It is no compensation to lavish praise on their shadowy anonymous author as "the greatest theologian in all history."

There is a deeper issue. Our author states:

He who saw it has borne *witness*—his testimony is *true*, and he knows that he tells the *truth*. (Jn 19:35, italics mine)

This author claims to have been a true witness, that is, an eyewitness, of Jesus. In his first letter he said that he and his fellows had "heard," "seen" and "touched" the "word of life" (1 Jn 1:1-2). His claims are extensive and specific.

The alternatives are simple. Either the writer was the truthful eyewitness he claims to have been, or, as Barrett and Brown believe, he was not. If Barrett and Brown are correct, the author was not in fact an eyewitness and not a disciple. Therefore it appears to me that he was not truthful at this point. If he was not truthful he cannot be a "great theologian," since theology is about God, who is truth. Although according to Barrett and Brown the fourth Evangelist is "the greatest theologian in history," he himself does not claim to be a theologian at all; he simply claims to be a special friend of Jesus and a true witness to his signs, his crucifixion and his risen person. The problem of his fundamental claim being incorrect is not really resolved by praising him at a point where he makes no claims. What cannot be denied is that all the evidence on the identity of the author, from both inside and outside the Fourth Gospel, points not to an unknown author but to John Zebedee, the beloved disciple.

Many scholars cannot believe that a member of Jesus' original circle of disciples could have written the Fourth Gospel. Their chief difficulty lies with the author's expansive style of writing and with the sophistication of his theology. The author, it is claimed, wrote later than the Synoptics and from outside the milieu of Palestine.

In the last decades, however, greater knowledge of the geography of Palestine, along with the results of archaeological work, has led others to believe that the author was, in fact, familiar with the countryside of both Galilee and Judea, and that he had an intimate knowledge of Jerusalem and the temple area.

Greater awareness of the difference in the ethos after the war in A.D. 66-70 has strengthened the case that the author wrote from the earlier, rather than the later, period. This is consistent with the book's own identification of its author as "the beloved disciple" and with the united opinion of second-century Christians, that "the beloved disciple" was John Zebedee.

What then of the expansive style and sophisticated theology? How could John Zebedee have been responsible for these? We reply that someone wrote this book and that it was written before the end of the first century. Are there substantial, as opposed to merely stylistic, grounds for doubting John Zebedee was that someone? His involvement with Jesus as one of the inner circle and his lengthy experience of leadership in the Jerusalem Christian community add to the strong probability that John Zebedee was in fact the author of the Fourth Gospel.

FURTHER READING

Archibald M. Hunter, *The Gospel According to John* (New York: Cambridge University Press, 1965).

Leon L. Morris, *Studies in the Fourth Gospel* (Grand Rapids: Eerdmans, 1969).

Stephen Smalley, *John, Evangelist and Interpreter* (Greenwood, S.C.: Attic Press, 1983).

WITNESS TWO

Peter Through Mark

Although the Second Gospel does not say who wrote it, Christians of the following century were in no doubt. Their unanimous opinion was that Mark wrote it on the basis of information supplied by Peter. Writing c. A.D. 110 at Hierapolis in Asia Minor, Papias, "a hearer of John" stated:

> Mark . . . having been the interpreter of Peter, wrote . . . all that he recalled of what was either said or done by the Lord. For he neither heard the Lord, nor was he a follower of his, but at a later date . . . of Peter. (quoted in Eusebius *Church History* 3.39)

This is also the view of Justin writing in Rome c. 150, of Irenaeus in Gaul c. 170 and of Clement in Alexandria c. 180.

But were Peter and Mark capable of writing the Gospel of Mark? Many modern scholars now believe this Gospel, despite its apparent simplicity, to be a skillfully written and profound piece of literature. Were humble folk like Peter and Mark capable of creating a document like this?

PETER AND JOHN MARK

Was Peter the poor and illiterate person he is often supposed to have been? In fact, he was involved in a fishing partnership (Lk 5:10), and, with his brother Andrew, he owned a house in Capernaum (Mk 1:29). His original name, Simon, is a Greek name; he came from Galilee of the Gentiles, a bilingual region. Since he was a person of at least modest means, he may be assumed to have been literate, as people from his socioeconomic class were usually educated to some degree.

Some time after Jesus' resurrection Peter moved to Jerusalem, where for ten years (c. 33-43) he was leader of the large Jerusalem Christian community and its spokesman both to the crowds (Acts 2:14-42; 3:12-26), and also to the high priests (Acts 4:8-12; 5:29-32). Doubtless some personal and intellectual development occurred as Peter moved from a fishing business in Capernaum to Jerusalem, the world capital of the Jewish people, where he engaged in such activities as leading, preaching and teaching (Acts 2:40, 42; 6:2).

During this period, however, Peter was not confined to Jerusalem; after the killing of Stephen and the scattering of the Christian Hellenists, Peter (with John Zebedee) traveled to Samaria (Acts 8:14-25) to check on and consolidate Philip's evangelism of the Samaritans. Later, he visited Christian groups in Lydda and Joppa (Acts 9:32-43), and probably others in the bilingual coastal strip from Azotus to Caesarea where Philip had been active (Acts 8:40). Eventually he came to Caesarea, the Roman garrison city where Philip had settled (Acts 8:40; 21:8) and spoke in the house of a senior Roman officer, Cornelius (Acts 10:24-48).

In c. 43 the leadership of the Jerusalem church passed to James, the Lord's brother, since Peter was forced to flee because of Herod Agrippa's persecutions (Acts 12:1-3, 17).

Nevertheless, he remained within the orbit of the Jerusalem church, being referred to as one of its "pillars," though by then (c. 47) his name was mentioned after that of James (Gal 2:9).

At the missionary "summit" meeting c. 47 (Gal 2:7-9) it was agreed that Peter, as well as James and John, should go to the Jews with the Christian message. This apparently is what Peter proceeded to do. We hear of him in Antioch c. 49 (Gal 2:11-14) and in Corinth c. 53 (1 Cor 1:12; 9:5). The first letter of Peter appears to have been written from Rome (1 Pet 5:13 "Babylon" = Rome) in the early sixties.

Peter's is a remarkable story. He began as an obscure fisherman in remote Capernaum and when last heard of was in Rome, the capital of the Empire. In the intervening three decades he accompanied Jesus in Galilee and Judea, led the church in Jerusalem, was an itinerant missionary leader in Palestine, and traveled as a missionary to the Jewish Diaspora in Syria, Greece and Italy. Is it really so incredible that someone with this breadth of experience, despite relatively humble origins, should provide the resource information for the Second Gospel?

What of John Mark? His mother's house was apparently a major meeting place for the Jerusalem church, or perhaps that part of it that looked to Peter's leadership as opposed to James (Acts 12:12-17; cf. Gal 1:18-19). Reference to "the house of Mary" suggests she was a widow; Mark's father is never mentioned. It was apparently a large house since "many were gathered together . . . praying" (Acts 12:12). The presence of a maid (Acts 12:13) adds to a picture of a substantial, possibly wealthy, establishment to which John Mark belonged. His two names, John (Hebrew) and Mark (Greek or Latin), together with a probably affluent background, make it likely that this man was educated and bilingual, with Greek as his second language.

John Mark was associated with famous leaders. He was a cousin of Barnabas (Col 4:10), whom he accompanied c. 50 on what was probably a missionary tour of Cyprus (Acts 15:39). Earlier, c. 47, he was the younger colleague of Barnabas and Paul for the first part of the missionary tour of Cyprus and southern Galatia (Acts 13:13). The dispute between Paul and John Mark (Acts 15:37-39) was subsequently resolved, since later Paul refers to him as a "fellow worker" (Philem 23) and as someone whose help he needed (2 Tim 4:11). Peter, writing from Rome c. 63, refers affectionately to Mark as "my son" (1 Pet 5:13), possibly reflecting a surrogate father relationship going back to Jerusalem in the thirties and forties.

The Gospel that bears Mark's name contains a detail that, significantly, is found in no other Gospel. At the arrest of Jesus in Jerusalem, "a young man followed him, with nothing but a linen cloth about his body; and they seized him, but he left the linen cloth and ran away naked" (Mk 14:51-52). This is, according to William Barclay, "an extraordinarily trivial and irrelevant incident to insert into the high tragedy of the events in the garden."[1] He quotes T. Zahn: "Mark paints a small picture of himself in the corner of his work." If Mark was in fact the "young man" of, shall we say, twenty years of age in the year c. 33, by the early sixties when many suppose him to have written his Gospel he would have been about fifty years old.

John Mark, then, was from a financially strong background, therefore educated and bilingual. He had been the close colleague of Barnabas, Paul and Peter, and by the time he was fifty years of age had worked as a missionary colleague with noted church leaders for a decade and a half.

Let us consider one further piece of information. In the prologue to his two-volume work, Luke acknowledges having received written information about Jesus from certain "ministers" before him, one of whom must have been the author of Mark, since so much of his Gospel is incorporated in the Gospel according to Luke. The Greek word for minister is *hypēretēs,* which is defined by Gerhard Kittle as "assistant to another as the instrument of his will" and is a word Luke used of John Mark on the first missionary tour. Barnabas and Paul "had John as *hypēretēs*"—as their minister or attendant. Is Luke identifying John Mark the *hypēretēs* (Acts 13:5) with the author of a text on which he came to rely (Lk 1:2)?

Our conclusion is that in terms of education and experience, Peter and John Mark could have written the Second Gospel, as second-century Christian writers claimed. But did they? Unfortunately, as we have seen, this Gospel does not state who wrote it, except perhaps to imply that the author was the "young man" in Jerusalem who fled naked into the darkness on the night Jesus was arrested. The one course of inquiry open to us is to decide whether or not the information contained in the Gospel and its manner of presentation is consistent with Petrine-Marcan authorship. If Peter were the source of the information Mark used, we would expect to discover biographical and historical elements. But do we find them?

PROCLAMATION OR HISTORY?

"The beginning of the gospel of Jesus Christ, the Son of God"—these are the words with which the second Evangelist commenced his scroll and which became its title. What he wrote is a "gospel," the only one of the four we call Gospels to call itself by that name. Elsewhere in the New Testament the "gospel" is "proclaimed" or "spoken"; this is the only case where it is *written.* The Gospel of Mark, therefore, is written proclamation, written gospel.

There are a number of summaries of the "proclaimed" gospel in the Acts of the Apostles, as, for example, when Peter spoke to Cornelius and his family in Caesarea (Acts 10:34-43). The chief points Peter made to them were:

- After the baptism which John the Baptist proclaimed
- God anointed Jesus of Nazareth with power
- So that he proclaimed the gospel, beginning in Galilee and throughout all Judea.
- God was with him as he went about healing all who were oppressed by the devil.
- The people of Jerusalem had him crucified
- But God raised him on the third day.

In 1932 C. H. Dodd noticed this summary of Peter's speech bears a close resemblance to the sequence and structure of the written "gospel," especially the Gospel of Mark. According to Dodd the written Gospel was an expanded version of the spoken gospel.

The second Evangelist wrote his Gospel for public church reading. This is clear from the author's instructions to the church reader to explain an obscure item ("let the reader understand" Mk 13:14). Is it relevant that two-thirds of the episodes in this Gospel are less than ten sentences long? Certainly the narrative is fast-moving and gripping, with a minimum of recorded speech. One of the most successful post-World War II London stage shows, which played nightly to full houses, consisted of a cast of one person whose only script was the text of Mark's Gospel. Though written, Mark's Gospel somehow remains "proclamation." Is it intended to arouse our passions and move our wills to believe in Jesus?

There is no way that it could be regarded merely as a "life of Jesus." The adult Jesus simply enters the story near the beginning and is the focus of attention in the episodes that follow. There is an almost complete absence of biographical detail such as his father's name, his birthplace, his education, his age or his appearance. The story is told with a high sense of drama, so that although Jesus would have visited Jerusalem for the Jewish feasts nine or ten times during the three-year period of his public life, this Evangelist has him going there only once—to die!

Is this Gospel, therefore, unbiographical and unhistorical? The answer is that, although it is primarily in the form of a "proclamation," there are also at least four historical elements that characterize the Gospel of Mark.

Overall historical context. The Gospel of Mark permits us to place Jesus within a recognizable historical context. He began his public life in Galilee after the famous prophet *John the Baptist* had been arrested (Mk 1:14). His mission, as well as that of his disciples, occurred during the period *Herod Antipas* was the tetrarch of Galilee and Peraea (6:14). He was tried by the Roman prefect of Judea, *Pontius Pilate,* and crucified by his decision (15:15). These three persons serve as historical markers for the ministry of Jesus in the Gospel of Mark, because they are well known in other historical sources—John in Josephus; Antipas in Josephus and Tacitus;[2] and Pilate in Philo, Josephus and Tacitus.

Mark and Josephus give different names for Herodias's former husband before she married Antipas (Mk 6:17; *Antiquities* 18.136),[3] but this is a relatively minor detail and does not detract from the overall dovetailing of Mark into a known historical context.

The Herodians. The Gospel of Mark refers to a group known as the Herodians,[4] who strongly opposed Jesus in both Galilee and Jerusalem (Mk 3:6; 12:13). Although scholars are uncertain about their exact composition and rationale, their historicity is not in question. It is significant that Mark's Gospel is the only primary source of historical information for this group. Matthew's only reference is clearly derived from Mark (Mt 22:16 = Mk 12:13). The Herodians are not mentioned in Luke or John.

Geographical details. The Gospel of Mark depicts Jesus as based in Capernaum (see also Mt 4:13) on the northern shore of Galilee, but it mentions that he increasingly needed to withdraw outside Galilee for various reasons and for apparently more and more lengthy periods.[5] While this is not made obvious by the author, careful reading makes it likely to have been the case.

After his initial and spectacular activities in Capernaum (Mk 1:28, 33) Jesus withdrew because of the crowds (1:37-38) to "all Galilee, preaching in their synagogues" (1:39).

Back in Capernaum (2:1) it became necessary to leave on account of the Pharisees' and Herodians' plot (3:6). He engaged in public ministry by the

Sea of Galilee (3:7) and went to an unidentified mountain for intensive teaching of the Twelve (3:13).

Again in Capernaum (3:19), after a dispute with scribes from Jerusalem, he withdrew to the seaside for public teaching (3:22—4:1). He stayed in the boat from which he had been speaking and traveled directly to the Decapolis (4:1, 35-36; 5:1). After they recrossed the sea to the town where Jairus lived (5:21-43), he visited Nazareth (6:1-6) and then visited the villages of Galilee (6:6).

When Jesus returned to Capernaum, he dispatched the Twelve for their village mission (6:7); they returned to him (6:30), followed by men from "all the towns" (6:33), their mission having come to the attention of Herod Antipas (6:14). Again he withdrew, taking his disciples with them, to the northeast side of the lake at or near Bethsaida (see Lk 9:10) where the people sought to make him king (see Jn 6:14-15).

Jesus is next found at Gennesaret in Galilee (Mk 6:53), from where he returned to Capernaum and became involved in a serious dispute with local Pharisees and Jerusalem scribes (7:1). Once more he left, and this time went to the districts of Tyre and Sidon on the distant coast of Phoenicia (7:24), and from there to the region of Decapolis (7:31), where he fed the four thousand (8:1-9).

Jesus' next visit to Galilee was brief. When he and the disciples went from the Decapolis to Dalmanutha (8:10), there was yet another dispute with the Pharisees (8:11-12), so they left immediately by boat for Bethsaida (8:13, 22), with Jesus warning the disciples of the "leaven of the Pharisees and . . . of Herod [Antipas]" (8:15), the two sources of opposition who kept forcing him out of Galilee. From Bethsaida they traveled to the northern and mountainous regions of Caesarea Philippi (8:27), near the source of the Jordan. Six days after Peter had declared Jesus to be "the Christ" (8:29), Jesus took three of the disciples to a "high mountain," (probably Mt. Hermon, close to two miles high and about twelve-and-a-half miles northeast of Caesarea Philippi), where the transfiguration occurred (9:2-8). From there they set out for Jerusalem, reentering Galilee, but in great secrecy (9:30), and returning to "the house" in Capernaum (9:33). Jesus and the Twelve then followed the Jordan valley (10:1), coming eventually to Jericho (10:46) and ultimately to Jerusalem (11:1, 11).

Thus the Gospel of Mark conveys a strong sense of extensive activity in Galilee, based in Capernaum but with periods of enforced withdrawal to neighboring regions to the west, east and north. Mark's account, told in terms of the persistent opposition of local and Jerusalem Pharisees and with the ever-present menace of the tetrarch Herod Antipas (and the Herodians), is expressed in terms of specific geographic movement inside and outside Galilee, and is therefore historically credible.

Linkages between episodes. The Gospel of Mark, despite the claims of some scholars that it is a haphazard collection of episodes with no developing story, does in fact contain a number of biographical and historical links between the episodes.

One example is the house in Capernaum that belonged to Simon (and his brother Andrew?) to which Jesus came (Mk 1:29) and where he initially stayed (1:33, 35-36). It was to this house that he returned after his various voluntary and enforced withdrawals from Capernaum (2:1; 3:19; [7:17]; 9:33). Evidently this house became his own home and his base of operations for ministry in greater Galilee and the regions outside Galilee.[6] These Capernaum "house" references, which span the various episodes for more than half the Gospel, are an indication that, in an overall way, the Gospel of Mark is historical in character.

Another example is Jesus' relationship with people in another town—his own town, Nazareth. He left Nazareth to be baptized by John in the Jordan River (Mk 1:9), some time after which he settled in Capernaum (1:29; cf. Mt 4:13). He is regularly referred to as "Jesus of Nazareth" (1:24; 10:47; 16:6) or as "the Nazarene, Jesus" (14:67). Apart from his visit to Nazareth after his baptism (Lk 4:16-30), he appears not to have returned there for some time. When he came back, the people of Nazareth were so skeptical (Mk 6:2) that he made his famous remark that "a prophet is not without honor, except in his own country" (6:4). Those who did not "honor" this prophet were those of "his own country" (district or region), "his own kin" (extended family) and "his own house" (immediate family, as in 6:3—Mary, his mother; his brothers James, Joses, Judas and Simon; and his sisters [who are not mentioned by name]). The skepticism of Nazareth was thoroughgoing, extending from his immediate family through the network of relatives to the wider community.

This skepticism in Nazareth was not new. Earlier "his family" (Mk 3:21), that is, his mother and brothers (3:31), set out from Nazareth to Capernaum to "seize" him (3:21) since they believed he was "out of his mind" (3:21 NRSV). On arrival they stood "outside" (3:31), presumably outside the house in Capernaum, whereupon Jesus commented that his (true) mother and brothers were those who did the will of God (3:35).

Here then is another linkage, spanning four chapters, indicating the consistent unbelief of the people of Nazareth, including his own family, as contrasted with the new "family" in Capernaum, based as it was on the house of Simon and Andrew. These two intersecting examples of references that span several episodes and chapters are evidence of the underlying historicity of the Gospel of Mark.

In conclusion we ask: does the written proclamation also have biographical and historical characteristics that would be consistent with Petrine-Marcan authorship? The evidence for an affirmative answer is that Mark's story dovetails into its historical context; that it refers to the existence of the "Herodians" group; that Jesus' withdrawals are consistent with the historical circumstances of Galilee and with its geography; and that certain subtle linkages between episodes imply that the narrative is founded on historical truth. But is there more that can be said?

EVIDENCE OF AN EYEWITNESS

In this section we will attempt to show that, in addition to information of a historical character, there are also traces of evidence that in all probability go back to an eyewitness.

Vivid detail. There are many examples of vivid detail in the Gospel of Mark. Where do they come from? Do they arise from the author's lively imagination or from his recollection of things that made an impression on his memory? If the examples were long descriptive passages we would be inclined to attribute them to his imagination. Since, however, they are confined to small details it is more likely that they arose from his recollection of striking and colorful events. Let us consider some examples.

> That evening, at *sundown . . . the whole city* was gathered together about [literally "facing"] *the door.* (1:32-33, italics mine)

The expectancy of the crowd facing the door at sundown has impressed the memory of an eyewitness. How else do we explain these words?

> When *evening* had come . . . leaving the crowd, they took him with them in the boat, *just as he was*. And *other boats* were with him. . . . [A]nd the waves beat into the boat, so that *the boat was already filling*. But he was in the stern, *asleep on the cushion*. (4:35-38, italics mine)

This passage reflects the emotions of horror and fear that Jesus was asleep when the boat was filling with water.

> A man . . . who lived among the tombs . . . had often been bound with fetters and chains, but the chains he *wrenched apart*, and the fetters he *broke in pieces*; and no one had the strength to subdue him. Night and day among the tombs and on the mountains he was always *crying out*, and *bruising* himself with *stones*. (5:2-5, italics mine)

Here is a grim picture of chains hanging from hands and legs and the bruised body as well as of the reports of weird nocturnal noises that imprinted itself upon the memory of someone who had been present.

> When they came to the house of the ruler of the synagogue, he *saw a tumult*, and people *weeping and wailing loudly*. . . . He said to them . . . "[T]he child is not dead but sleeping." And they *laughed at him*. . . . Taking her by the hand he said to her, *"Talitha cumi."* (5:38-41, italics mine)

The Aramaic words stand out against the memory of the sounds of wailing and scornful laughter as the very words used by Jesus to the dead child.

> He commanded them all to sit down by companies upon the *green grass*. So [the people] sat down in *groups* [literally as "garden beds"], by *hundreds* and by *fifties*. (6:39-40, italics mine)

This is almost a photographic image of people sitting in groups, their colorful robes giving the appearance of flower beds set in green grass.

These words of Mark leap from the page. To my mind they can only have come from the memory of someone who was struck by the drama of the scene or its color or sound or strangeness. Behind these words are the recollections of someone who had been present.

The emotions of Jesus. Prominent among the vivid details in Mark's Gospel are Jesus' emotional and personal responses in particular situations. How do we account for these in the Gospel? Are they the result of the author's imagination or of his recollection? The author does not systematically develop them, and there is no sign that they have been contrived in any way. Rather, the writer mentions them in passing. Some examples are listed below.

- A leper came to him. . . . *Moved with pity,* [Jesus] stretched out his hand and touched him. . . . And he *sternly charged* him, and sent him away. (Mk 1:40-43, italics mine)

- A man was there who had a withered hand. And they watched . . . whether he would heal him on the sabbath. . . . And he looked around at them with *anger, grieved* at their hardness of heart, and said to the man, "Stretch out your hand." (Mk 3:1-2, 5, italics mine)

- The apostles returned to Jesus. . . . And *he said* to them, *"Come away by yourselves to a lonely place, and rest a while."* . . . As he went ashore he saw a great throng, and he had *compassion* on them, because they were like sheep without a shepherd. (6:30-34, italics mine)

- Immediately he *made* [= compelled] his disciples get into the boat and go before him to the other side. (6:45, italics mine)

- And they were bringing children to him, that he might touch them; and the disciples rebuked them. But when Jesus saw it he was *indignant,* and said to them, "Let the children come to me." . . . And he took them in his arms and blessed them, laying his hands upon them. (10:13-14, 16, italics mine)

- A man ran up and knelt before him, and asked. . . . And Jesus looking upon him *loved* him. (10:17, 21, italics mine)

- *And he took with him Peter and James and John, and began to be greatly *distressed and troubled.* And he said . . . "My soul is very sorrowful, even to death." (14:33-34, italics mine)

- "Elo-i, Elo-i, lama sabach-thani?" which means "My God, my God, why hast thou *forsaken* me?" (15:34, italics mine)

How else do we explain these references to the intensely human and emotional behavior of Jesus—his compassion, his anger, his fatigue, his concern for others, his indignation, his love, his dread, his sense of abandonment—than as reactions which registered strongly with someone who was present at the time? It seems unlikely that such references arose out of an author's imagination.

On five occasions this author mentions that Jesus "looked around" (as in a circle): in the synagogue when they watched if he would heal on the Sabbath (3:5); in the house in Capernaum with his mother and brothers outside (3:34); at the crowd, to see who touched him (5:32); to the disciples when he said how hard it was for the wealthy to enter the kingdom of God (10:23); and on his arrival in the temple (11:11). This "look" that occurred on dramatic occasions is not recorded by Matthew and only once by Luke. Underlying Mark's account is the memory of someone who saw—and was deeply impressed by—the way Jesus "looked around" at these times of high drama.

"They" passages. In 1928 C. H. Turner, in his commentary on Mark, noticed that the second Evangelist often used they in his narrative, speaking of the disciples, whereas Matthew and Luke frequently omit them, referring only to Jesus and the other person in the story. Mindful of Papias's statement that Mark wrote what he heard from Peter, Turner suggested that Peter must have often said "we," speaking for himself and the other disciples present with Jesus. Since Mark was not present with Peter and the others, he cannot write "we"; he must write "they." When Matthew and Luke take over Mark's material the word *they* drops out, leaving the singular *he*, Jesus. Thus, in Turner's reconstruction, the process was

Peter's teaching of component stories	⟶	Mark's writing of component stories	⟶	Matthew and Luke supplementing and adapting Mark
We + Jesus + person(s) in story		*They* + Jesus + person(s) in story		Jesus + person(s) in story

There are many of Mark's stories in which we can easily imagine the "they" having originally been, from Peter's mouth as "we," for example:

And immediately he left the synagogue and entered the house of Simon and Andrew, with James and John. . . . Simon's [my] mother-in-law lay sick with a fever, and immediately they [we] told him of her. And he came and took her by the hand. (Mk 1:29-31).

Note that Matthew 8:14-15 has removed all plurals while Luke 4:38-39 has altered two of the three plurals. Other examples in Mark's Gospel are:

And they [we] came to Bethsaida. And some people brought to him a blind man. (8:22)

They [we] went on from there and passed through Galilee. And he would not have any one know it. (9:30)

And they [we] came to Jerusalem. And he entered the temple. (11:15)

While it is not possible to prove Papias's statement that Mark was the "interpreter of Peter" (a statement with which every second-century writer who ventures an opinion on the authorship of the second Gospel agrees), the internal evidence is quite consistent with that statement. While the C. H. Turner view must remain as no more than an interesting possibility, it seems to me that the vivid details and the references to the emotions of Jesus demand that behind the written text lies the testimony of an eyewitness.

JESUS IN JERUSALEM

The Gospel of Mark has sixteen chapters, no less than six of which are devoted to what happened to Jesus in Jerusalem. In terms of actual words, Mark devotes approximately one-third of his Gospel to the events of those few days in Jerusalem. It may be significant that these chapters are very precise and detailed in matters of *time, place* and *people*. The table on page 87 gives examples of Mark's time and place details.

Details of people. Apart from those disciples who are named and the Roman prefect, Pontius Pilate, Mark mentions the following by name: Barabbas, a murderer who had taken part in "the insurrection" (15:6-15); Simon of Cyrene, "the father of Alexander and Rufus" (15:21); Mary Magdalene, also "Mary the mother of James the younger and of Joses," and "Salome" (15:40; 16:1); and Joseph of Arimathea (15:43-46).

Details of time

And he entered Jerusalem, and went into the temple. . . . [I]t was already *late*. (Mk 11:11, italics mine)

On the *following* day . . . (11:12)

As they passed by in *the morning* . . . (11:20)

And they came *again* to Jerusalem. (11:27)

It was now *two days* before the Passover. (14:1)

And on the *first day* of Unleavened Bread . . . (14:12)

And when it *was evening* . . . (14:17)

And as soon as it *was morning* . . . (15:1)

And it was the *third* hour. (15:25)

And when the *sixth* hour had come . . . (15:33)

And when *evening* had come . . . (15:42)

And when the *sabbath was past* . . . (16:1)

Details of place

They drew near to *Jerusalem*, to *Bethphage and Bethany*, at the *Mount of Olives*. (Mk 11:1; cf. 11:15, 27; 14:16, italics mine)

He went out to *Bethany*. (11:11; cf. 14:3)

And as he came out of the *Temple* . . . (13:1)

And as he sat on the *Mount of Olives* opposite the temple . . . (13:3; cf. 14:26)

And they went to a place which was called *Gethsemane*. (14:32)

And Peter had followed him at a distance, right into the *courtyard of the high priest*. (14:54)

And the soldiers led him away inside the *palace* (that is, the *praetorium*). (15:16)

And they brought him to the place called *Golgotha*. . . . And they crucified him. (15:22, 24)

And he [Joseph of Arimathea] . . . laid him in a [his] *tomb* which had been hewn out of the rock. (15:46)

Since there are so many details in those last six chapters, it has been suggested that they originally existed separately as the earliest part of the Gospel to assume written form. This part of Mark's Gospel refers five times to the high priest (14:53, 54, 60, 61, 63) without mentioning his name. This has been taken to imply that Caiaphas was still the high priest when the story was being written, there being no need to mention his name. Since Caiaphas was high priest until A.D. 37, it is possible that this Jerusalem Gospel came into being before that date.

As to the author, we conjecture that if Peter was at that stage associated with the home of John Mark (see Acts 12:12-17), it is quite possible that this part of the Gospel arose from the collaborative effort of Peter and Mark back in the middle thirties.

Upon examination, the Gospel of Mark is found to be consistent with Papias's statement that Mark used Peter as his source. Looked at as a whole, this Gospel corresponds with Peter's preaching outline as in the speech to Cornelius. Considered in its component parts, it is found to be rich in historical information and vivid detail, supporting the proposition that an eyewitness wrote, or was the source of, the Gospel of Mark.

FURTHER READING

William Barclay, *The Gospels and Acts,* vol. 1 (London: SCM Press, 1976).

C. H. Dodd, *The Apostolic Preaching and Its Developments* (Grand Rapids: Baker, 1980).

Ralph P. Martin, *Mark, Evangelist and Theologian* (Grand Rapids: Zondervan, 1973).

Hugo Staudinger, *The Trustworthiness of the Gospels* (Edinburgh: Handsel Press, 1981).

LUKE AND MATTHEW

N ow that we have discussed the Gospels by John and Mark, we turn to the two remaining Evangelists, Luke and Matthew.

LUKE

From the second half of the second century, Christian writers are unanimous about two matters.

First, they attribute the third Gospel to Luke, the physician who accompanied Paul on his journeys. Thus the Muratorian Canon written from Rome c. A.D. 190 states:

> The third book of the gospel, that according to Luke, was compiled in his own name on Paul's authority by Luke the Physician, when after Christ's ascension Paul had taken him to be with him . . . yet neither did he see the Lord in the flesh.[1]

Similarly, Irenaeus, writing from Gaul c. 170, declared: "Luke . . . the companion of Paul, recorded in a book the gospel preached by him" (*Against Heresies* 3.1.1).

Irenaeus describes how a heretic treated the Gospel of Luke in the early 140s:

> Marcion . . . mutilates the gospel which is according to Luke, removing all that is written respecting the generation of the Lord, and sets aside a great deal of the teaching of the teachings of the Lord. (*Against Heresies* 3.1.1)

According to these authorities, the writer of the third Gospel was Luke, Paul's companion.

Second, those early writers were convinced that Luke was not an eyewitness. One example will suffice—the Muratorian Canon says:

> Yet neither did he [Luke] see the Lord in the flesh; and he too, as he was able to ascertain events, begins his story from the birth of John.[2]

Luke's Gospel begins this way:

> Inasmuch as many have undertaken to compile a narrative of the things which have been accomplished among us, just as they were delivered to us by those who from the beginning were eyewitnesses and ministers of the word, it seemed good to me also . . . to write an orderly account for you, most excellent Theophilus, that you may know the truth concerning the things of which you have been informed. (1:1-4)

From this we infer the following:

1. Certain people had compiled "narratives" about Jesus.

2. The eyewitnesses of Jesus "delivered" these to Luke, who was not an eyewitness.

3. Using these, Luke has written up a comprehensive history.

What were these "narratives" and who were these "eyewitnesses"? If Luke has woven together certain strands as they were "delivered" to him, it may be possible for us to unravel and examine each of them. This is the science called source criticism. It tells us that Luke used the following three strands:

1. Mark's Gospel. Luke incorporates approximately 50 percent of Mark, which represents about 25 percent of Luke's total.

2. The nativity stories (chapters 1 and 2; about 10 percent of Luke's total).

3. A document known as Proto-Luke (chapters scattered through Luke but especially 9—18 and 22—24). Proto-Luke was a document thought to be in existence earlier than Mark and composed of Q—a collection of sayings of Jesus referred to by scholars as Q (*Quelle* is German for

"source")—and L, which is made up of (a) narrative (Zacchaeus, trial before Herod), (b) miracles (healing of ten lepers) and (c) parables (good Samaritan, prodigal son).

Let us leave for the moment the historical significance of these strands in Luke and the use he makes of them.

MATTHEW

Although the Gospel according to Matthew was the most widely used, its origins are shrouded in mystery. The title of the Gospel, which was in use by the middle of the second century, is intended to identify the author as Matthew, that is, Levi the tax collector, one of the twelve disciples (Mt 9:9 = Mk 2:14 = Lk 5:27). References to Matthew from the second century are not numerous. Irenaeus c. 170 wrote:

Matthew also issued a written gospel among the Hebrews in their own dialect. (*Against Heresies* 3.1.1)

Papias c. 130 had commented:

Matthew compiled the oracles in the Hebrew language: but everyone interpreted them as he was able.[3]

As it is likely that Irenaeus merely echoes Papias, probably we have not two sources but one. Two things are clear from these references. First, the author was one of the twelve disciples. Second, he compiled the sayings of Jesus in Hebrew. The source critics have discovered three basic strands in Matthew:

1. Mark's Gospel. Matthew reproduces 90 percent of Mark's material, which represents about 50 percent of Matthew's total.

2. The source known as Q, which Luke also reproduces (as part of Proto-Luke), representing about 25 percent of Matthew's total.

3. Material found only in Matthew, usually known as M, representing about 25 percent of Matthew's total.

Difficulties have been found with Irenaeus's and Papias's comments about Matthew's Gospel. Why, for example, would an eyewitness need someone else's narrative (Mark's) when he could write his own? How can

Papias claim Matthew "compiled oracles in the Hebrew language" when the Gospel as we have it is written in Greek? What are the answers to these important questions?

One possible solution is that Matthew originally wrote Q or perhaps the collection of Old Testament quotations in Hebrew. In this case Matthew, or some other writer unknown to us, subsequently translated these "Hebrew oracles" into Greek and combined them with Mark and the other source(s), thus completing the Gospel in its present form. But who the final author/editor was, and by what processes he gathered his sources, are matters about which there is no certain information.

What can be stated is that the Gospel was in use at least by the eighties and that the author made use of the three sources Mark, Q and M.

MARK IN MATTHEW AND LUKE

Luke and Matthew both incorporate preexistent strands and weave them together into their respective Gospels. Earlier we saw that the other two Evangelists, John and Mark, appear to be their own sources, John having been an eyewitness, Mark the companion of an eyewitness.

The use of earlier sources by Matthew and Luke has great significance for the question of the trustworthiness of these two writers. Of the four strands—Mark, Q, M, L—that Matthew and Luke use, Mark exists independently and Q is reproduced in both. We are immediately able to check the accuracy and the integrity of Matthew and Luke by their use of preexistent sources, in particular their use of Mark. What do we discover?

Let us investigate a particular case, part of the parable of the wicked tenants.

Mark 12:5-7	Matthew 21:36-38	Luke 20:12-14
And he sent another, and him they killed; and so with many others, some they beat and some they killed.	Again he sent other servants, more than the first; and they did the same to them.	And he sent yet a third; this one they wounded and cast out.

Mark 12:5-7	Matthew 21:36-38	Luke 20:12-14
He had still one other, a beloved son; finally he sent him to them, saying, "They will respect my son."	Afterward he sent his son to them, saying, "They will respect my son."	Then the owner of the vineyard said, "What shall I do? I will send my beloved son; it may be they will respect him."
But those tenants said to one another,	But when the tenants saw the son, they said to themselves,	But when the tenants saw him, they said to themselves,
"This is the heir; come, let us kill him, and the inheritance will be ours."	"This is the heir; come, let us kill him and have his inheritance."	"This is the heir; let us kill him, that the inheritance may be ours."

Two comments may be made. First, Matthew and Luke do not follow Mark slavishly. Both authors tell the story with fewer (Greek) words (Mark: fifty; Luke: forty-seven; Matthew: forty-five) and with more polished expression. After an exhaustive comparison of Matthew's and Luke's use of Mark, Edwyn Clement Hoskyns and Francis Noel Davey wrote:

> The authors of the two later gospels are concerned for their Greek readers. They add, in order to make clear what Jesus demands of his disciples. They simplify, in order to avoid crude misunderstanding. They omit what appears to be trivial and unnecessary. They order and arrange the tradition, in order that it may be the more easily read in public or in private, and they improve the grammar and style, in order that their intelligent readers may not be unreasonably provoked.[4]

Second, Jesus' statement about himself that he is the sender's (that is, God's) "beloved son" is one of the most important theological statements in Mark. What do Matthew and Luke do with it? Luke reproduces it as it is, but Matthew actually omits "beloved," thus weakening the impact. Not that Matthew has a low view of Jesus: he is "Emmanuel . . . God with us" (Mt 1:23), the Son who alone knows the Father (Mt 11:27). Yet, so far from expanding, elevating or magnifying the "Son" at this point, Matthew reduces him for some reason. This example is typical of the way Luke and Matthew use Mark. Hoskyns and Davey commented:

> But in the whole of this process of editing they nowhere heighten Mark's tremendous conception of Jesus. No deifying of a prophet or of a mere preacher of righteousness can be detected.[5]

When we make a close scrutiny of Matthew and Luke at work on the text of Mark we discover them to be careful scribes who do not exaggerate the claims of Jesus in the way they present them. Luke's sober care may also be discerned in the account of the raising of the dead son of the widow of Nain, which is found only in Luke's Gospel (7:11-17). The setting is one of profound tragedy. A woman who is without a husband has now lost her only son. She is left without visible means of support. Her family line is at an end. When Jesus saw the funeral procession near the city gate, he was moved with compassion and raised the boy to life again. Luke records the amazement of the onlookers and the sentiments they expressed. He could easily have had them say that "this was the Son of God" or "God was with them" or some other utterance to present an exalted view of Jesus. In fact Luke has not heightened the Christology as he might so easily have done as the one who also wrote the Acts of the Apostles, where the postresurrection glory of Jesus is so important. Luke gives us instead the relatively mild verbal reaction of the onlookers. They said Jesus was a "great prophet," and that is all.

EARLIER SOURCES AS EYEWITNESSES

Since at the point where we can check them—namely, in their work on Mark, Matthew and Luke—they prove trustworthy, we are encouraged about their use of the other sources at their disposal.[6] Q is a substantial source that scholars study in its own right. It has its own distinctive structure, style and theological emphasis. Similarly, the contents and emphases of the other sources may also be scrutinized, though it is beyond the scope of this book to do so. What is clear from the First and Third Gospels is that the following sources were already in existence and by an early date:

- Mark
- Q
- M
- The Infancy Stories (Luke)
- Proto-Luke (Q + L)

These sources emanate from either individuals or churches and as such they represent further independent evidence for Jesus.

THE STYLES OF LUKE AND MATTHEW

Although Matthew and Luke both make use of the Gospel of Mark as well as Q, their Gospels are stylistically distinctive and aimed at different sets of readers. Neither Gospel is a simple variation of the other. The author of the Gospel of Matthew was a Jew who wrote for Jewish readers. Matthew did not need to explain, for example, what a phylactery was;[7] his Jewish audience already knew. Greater knowledge of the Jewish Talmud by Christian scholars has shown that in his presentation of the genealogy of Christ, his method of quoting the Old Testament as well as his way of telling the stories about Jesus, Matthew is thoroughly Semitic. Matthew wrote about Christ from and for the Jewish culture of his time.

Luke, on the other hand, wrote for readers who were educated and cultured Gentiles. Compare, for example, the prologue of Luke's second volume with the second volume of one of Josephus's works:

Acts 1:1 (NIV)	*Against Apion* 2.1
In my former book, Theophilus, I wrote about all that Jesus began to do and to teach.	In the first volume of my work, my most esteemed Epaphroditus, I demonstrated the antiquity of our race.

The similarities are striking. Both authors refer back to an earlier volume, briefly stating its contents; both dedicate their books to individuals whom they mention by name. Details such as these were literary conventions in vogue among educated Gentiles that Luke and Josephus both observed.

Clearly, then, Matthew and Luke belonged to separate cultural groups,

groups to which they addressed their Gospels respectively. In assessing the competence of Matthew or Luke as historians it would be unfair to compare them with either modern biographers or with one another. If comparison is to be made, it must be with other writers from the cultural group to which each belonged.

THE CHARACTER OF THE SOURCE STRANDS

Are these source strands historical in character? We would possibly expect them not to be, since they consist mostly of isolated teachings of Jesus with only the L source supplying any significant narrative information. It is interesting to compare these Synoptic source strands in their original form with the Mishnah, a collection of the sayings of the rabbis written more than a century after the Gospels. These sayings of the rabbis, which relate to legal and ethical matters within Judaism, contain virtually no details embedded within them that might indicate where or when or under what circumstances they were originally uttered. The source strands of the Synoptic Gospels, on the other hand, do contain some historical specifics, which are, however, mostly related to geographic details. Let us consider some examples.

The Q source. The Q source mentions that, after his baptism "Jesus returned from the Jordan" (Lk 4:1 = Mt 4:1) and that later he "entered into Capernaum" (Lk 7:1 = Mt 8:5). In a famous teaching passage, Jesus pronounced woes upon the northern cities of Chorazin, Bethsaida and Capernaum (Lk 10:13-15 = Mt 11:21-23), which the Twelve visited during their mission.

The M source. The geographic references in M are but few, being confined to Capernaum (Mt 17:24), Jerusalem (21:10) and "Galilee . . . a mountain" (28:16). Jesus instructed his disciples not to visit Gentile areas or any city of the Samaritans (10:5).

The L source. The relatively greater historical interest of Luke is evident in the L source, which in all probability he compiled. He stated that the ministry of John the Baptist commenced in the "fifteenth year of . . . Tiberius Caesar [A.D. 28 or 29], Pontius Pilate being governor of Judaea, and Herod [Antipas] being tetrarch of Galilee and his brother Philip tetrarch of the region of Ituraea and Trachonitis and Lysanias tetrarch of Abilene, in the high priesthood of Annas and Caiaphas" (Lk 3:1-2). This detailed statement, which mentions the Roman emperor and his local governor as well as the Jewish tetrarchs and high priests, is corroborated as accurate by external sources. In addition, L refers to such places as Nazareth (Lk 4:16), the lake of Gennesaret (5:1), a city called Nain (7:11), "passing between Samaria and Galilee" (17:11), Jericho (19:1), Jerusalem (19:11), the Mount of Olives (19:37) and a village named Emmaus (24:13).

The L strand also mentions a number of people by name—for example, Mary Magdalene, Joanna, "the wife of Chuza, Herod's steward" and Susanna (Lk 8:2-3); Martha and Mary (10:38-39); Zacchaeus, "a chief tax collector" (19:2); and Cleopas (24:18).

While the source strands vary between the relative simplicity of M to the historical sophistication of L, their historical character is evident, especially when one bears in mind the sayings of the Mishnah for which there is an almost total lack of historical "landmarks."

Two things can be said with confidence about Matthew and Luke. First, as we check their use of Mark we find that Matthew and Luke are responsible scribes who do not exaggerate the material at their disposal. Second, we discover, hidden within their Gospels, strands that existed before Matthew and Luke wrote, as sources of information about Jesus. The evidence for what Jesus did and said is significantly more extensive and complex than we might suspect from the four Gospels as they stand.

FURTHER READING

William Barclay, *The Gospels and Acts,* vol. 1 (London: SCM Press, 1976).

Edwyn Clement Hoskyns and Noel Davey, *The Riddle of the New Testament* (Geneva, Ala.: A. R. Allenson, 1947).

I. Howard Marshall, ed., *New Testament Interpretation* (Grand Rapids: Eerdmans, 1978).

Ralph P. Martin, *New Testament Foundations,* vol. 1 (Grand Rapids: Eerdmans, 1975).

10

The Birth of Jesus

Our two eyewitness sources, John and Mark, say nothing about the birth and boyhood of Jesus, although they refer to his mother and siblings (Mk 6:3; cf. 3:31; Jn 6:42; 7:3, 5, 10). It is only as an adult at the threshold of his ministry that John and Mark introduce Jesus to their readers.

The New Testament letters, including Paul's, are silent about the details of Jesus' birth and upbringing.

Our only information comes from Matthew and Luke. But is it trustworthy? What if these authors have contrived the birth stories as an introduction to an otherwise already completed story? Maybe the nativity stories are pious fiction and nothing more? This is certainly what some people think.

Perhaps church people have themselves fostered the idea—no doubt unintentionally. It sometimes seems that aesthetics rather than truth predominate in the Christian celebrations of Christmas. The rich tradition of Christmas music, combined with the sentiment of the occasion, often all but obliterate the question of historical reality. If baby Jesus has been reduced in the minds of many to the same level of mythological unreality as Santa Claus, do we Christians have anyone but ourselves to blame?

Let me give two reasons for confidence in the truth of the stories that deal with the birth of Jesus.

The Agreement of Matthew and Luke

There can be no doubt that Matthew and Luke wrote independently of each other. Matthew, as he wrote his scroll, did not have Luke's before him, nor did Luke have Matthew's. The difference of style and content make that clear. There can be no suggestion of copying or dependence of the one upon the other.

Yet these authors innocently agree at a number of critical points. In both Gospels Jesus is born in *Bethlehem*. This, apparently, is not a detail that was widely known. On one occasion recorded by John, the crowd specifically rejected Jesus as Messiah because he was a Galilean. "The Christ . . . comes from Bethlehem," they said (Jn 7:42), accurately quoting the ancient prophet (Mic 5:2). The manner in which John recounts the incident shows that he knew, even if others did not, that Jesus was born in Bethlehem.

Both Matthew and Luke indicate that Joseph, the legal father, is a *descendant of King David* (Mt 1:6-16; Lk 1:27, 32). Though Mark makes no mention of Joseph, John twice refers to Jesus as "son of Joseph" (1:45; 6:42). Nevertheless, Mark clearly teaches that Jesus is the "son of David" (Mk 10:47-48; 11:10; 12:35-37), something that John also knows, but makes nothing of (Jn 7:42).

In both Matthew and Luke, Mary the mother of Jesus was a *virgin* when she conceived him (Mt 1:18; Lk 1:35). In quite a subtle way John also appears to betray knowledge of the virgin birth in his reference to the Christians' spiritual *rebirth*: "children of God; who were born, not of blood nor of the will of the flesh nor of the will of man, but of God" (Jn 1:12-13). These words also describe the manner of the conception of Jesus of Nazareth, which occurred independently of "blood," "the will of the flesh" or "the will of man" but which depended directly upon God.

Matthew and Luke also agree as to when Jesus was born. *It was during the time* (37 B.C. to 4 B.C.) *when Herod the Great was king of Israel* (Mt 2:1; Lk 1:5, 24-26). These impressive points of agreement, which are uncontrived, are the more compelling when we consider the difference of perspective and emphasis in the two accounts. For his part, Luke shows the reader that Elizabeth, mother of John the Baptist, and Mary were cousins. He tells us that the angel's name was Gabriel. Matthew mentions neither of these details. Luke states that it was for some kind of registration or census that Joseph and Mary came from Nazareth to Bethlehem. Matthew, by contrast, implies that Joseph and Mary returned to settle in Nazareth in Galilee only after their escape to, and refuge in, Egypt (2:22). Matthew refers to the visit of the wise men, the jealousy of Herod, the slaughter of the children and the flight into Egypt, and he tells of the resettlement of Galilee because of Archelaus who had succeeded his father Herod in Judea. Luke is silent on these details.

The differences in the narratives indicate that not only were Matthew and Luke isolated from each other when they wrote, but also that the sources on which they depended were quite separate. Yet from these underlying independent source strands, we have detailed agreement about where Jesus was born, when, to which parents and the miraculous circumstances of his conception.

It may be agreed that Luke has been influenced by certain narratives from the Old Testament as to the form in which his stories are told. The account of the conception of John the Baptist is similar to the account of the conception of Samson (Lk 1:5-7; cf. Judg 13:2-5), while Mary's song of praise resembles Hannah's song (Lk 1:46-55; cf. 1 Sam 2:1-10). This means only that Luke has consciously modeled his style, and Mary her song, on certain parts of the Old Testament in order to show their belief that the same God was active in their affairs, as he was in former times. The facts about which Matthew and Luke agree, both innocently and independently, leave little doubt that we are dealing with history and reality and not pious fiction.

THE STORIES ARE CONSISTENT WITH KNOWN HISTORY

Some years ago, when researching the broad stream of Jewish history during the times of Herod the Great, I was struck by the way several aspects of the birth stories fit in. Fortunately in the Jewish historian Josephus we have an extensive source for the last years of Herod the King. A good way to get a feel for the period is to read relevant sections of his *Jewish War* and *Jewish Antiquities*.

Our dating system. Since Herod died in 4 B.C., Jesus must have been born in 7 or 6 B.C. to satisfy the detail of the search for boys two years old (Mt 2:16). Thus the year 2000 was really 2006 or 2007! Why is our anno Domini calendar incorrect? It is because the sixth-century monk Dionysius, when reforming the Roman calendar along Christian lines to pivot around the birth of Jesus, miscalculated the date of the death of Herod relative to the founding of Rome, the previous starting point for Western calendars.

Which census? A problem in Luke's account is that Jesus was born during the reign of Herod who died 4 B.C. (Lk 1:5; cf. Mt 1—2) while Luke himself locates the nativity to the time Quirinius was governor of Syria (Lk 2:2). The problem is that Quirinius did not become governor until A.D. 6-9 and the only census we know of occurred in A.D. 6-7. On the face of it Luke has contradicted himself and is about ten years astray. The birth of Jesus occurred before the death of Herod in about 7 or 6 B.C., not A.D. 6!

Various solutions have been proposed. The suggestion that Quirinius was also governor of Syria in Herod's day has no support from history. There are two main options. One is that Luke made an error. If so, however, the error may have been embedded in the sources on which he relied. The other option is that some kind of a census not known to us had been instituted in Herod's latter years. There is a parallel example of a census in the kingdom of Cappadocia ruled by Archelaus, a relative of Herod's (Tacitus *Annals* 6.41). Luke's wording, "This was the first census that took place while Quirinius was governor of Syria" (Lk 2:2 NIV) could equally be translated, "This was a census *before* Quirinius was governor of Syria." Some explanation along these lines is preferable to attributing an error of this magnitude to Luke. Given his pinpoint precision in dating the commencement of John the Baptist's ministry to the fifteenth year of Tiberius's rule (Lk 3:1-2), an error of the kind implied by Luke 2:2 seems unlikely.

Magi from the east. The "wise men [Greek: *magoi*] from the East" (Mt 2:1) most likely can be identified with astrologers from Mesopotamia, the ancient home of the science-cum-superstition of "stargazing." A large community of Jews also lived there.

A star. One of the great prophecies of the Old Testament, which would affect not only the Jews but also the whole world, concerned a star. According to Numbers 24:17,

a star shall come forth out of Jacob,
and a scepter shall rise out of Israel.

Centuries before Christ, the Jews interpreted this to mean that from the Jewish people would arise a ruler of the whole world. The Greek translation of the Old Testament for example, translates Numbers 24:17 as,

a star shall come forth out of Jacob, a *man* shall arise . . .

A hundred years after Christ, Rabbi Akiba saw ben Kosiba as that star who would rule the world. Akiba renamed him bar Kokhba, "son of a star." The Gentiles also knew of this Jewish prophecy. Both Tacitus and Suetonius refer to it. Tacitus, for example, writes of "a mysterious prophecy . . . of the ancient scriptures of their priests" whereby "the Orient would triumph and from Judaea would go forth *men* destined to rule the world" (*Histories* 5:13).

Tacitus changed the prophecy from the singular "man" to the plural "men," seeing the fulfillment in father and son Vespasian and Titus who, as the Roman victors of the Jews in A.D. 66-70, were both destined to become emperors. It is probable that a version of this prophecy was known by the *magoi* from Mesopotamia.

Every 805 years the planets Jupiter and Saturn draw near to each other. Astronomers have calculated that in 7 B.C. the two planets were conjoined three times—in May, September and December, and that in February, 6 B.C., they were joined by Mars, presenting a spectacular triangular conjunction.[1] It appears likely that the *magoi*, knowing the ancient star prophecy, on seeing the brilliant planetary formation, decided to visit Judea to see the new king of the world. Incidentally, the biblical record does not say there were three *magoi*.

In 1871 the astronomer John Williams published his authoritative list of sightings of comets. Comet number 52 on Williams's list appeared for seventy days early in 5 B.C. and would have been visible in the Middle East. Was this the "star" that guided the *magoi*? Why did Herod kill the boys who were two years old and younger? Could this figure be explained by the time in 7-6 B.C. when the conjunction of the stars appeared?

Time magazine, in its cover story of December 27, 1976, commented that while "there are those who dismiss the star as nothing more than a metaphor . . . others take the Christmas star more literally, and not without reason. Astronomical records show that there were several significant celestial events around the time of Jesus' birth."

Slaughter of innocents. Herod's paranoia in ordering the killing of the baby boys of Bethlehem is in character. Earlier in his reign the king had murdered his wife Mariamne. More recently, he had removed two sons, prompting Augustus's grim joke (see below) that it was safer to be Herod's pig than Herod's son. The king was scrupulous not to break the Old Testament ban on eating pig meat but he cared little about the sixth commandment.

Later, knowing his own death was close, Herod ordered the arrest of the distinguished men from every village of Judea. They were herded together in the Hippodrome in Jerusalem. Herod ordered, "The moment I expire have them . . . massacred; so shall all Judaea and every household weep for me, whether they will or no" (Josephus *Jewish War* 1.660).

The order was not carried out. But the incident shows that the one who was capable of issuing it was also capable of "the slaughter of the innocents."

There is a possible reference to the slaughter of the baby boys in the fourth-century-A.D. pagan writer Macrobius, who describes the reaction of the emperor Augustus to news from Palestine that had recently come to him:

> When he [Augustus] heard that Herod king of the Jews had ordered all the boys in Syria under the age of two years to be put to death and that the king's son was among those killed, he said, "I'd rather be Herod's pig *[hus]* than Herod's son *[huios]*."[2]

Unfortunately we don't know Macrobius's source or sources of information. It appears that he has fused two separate episodes into one—the killing of the baby boys and Herod's murder of a son of his own, who was then an adult and removed in circumstances different from those of the children. It does not seem that Macrobius merely quotes Matthew's story, since he was a convinced pagan and the reference to Syria is at odds with Matthew's version. It is more likely that the killing of the boys was recorded in a pagan source, now lost to us, but preserved in Macrobius. This extract may provide striking confirmation of Matthew's account that Herod the King ordered the killing of male children two years and younger.

Reliable stories. Are the stories about the birth of Jesus historically reliable? Enough has been written, I believe, to indicate it to be reasonable to accept their historicity. Matthew and Luke, though clearly independent of each other, agree on the major details of when and where it occurred, as well as the miraculous conception of the child. Moreover, many incidental details in the stories fit unobtrusively yet consistently into the known background of Jewish history.

But a word of caution: see Christ as he was through the sober lenses of the Gospels, not through the rose-colored glasses of popular Christmas tradition.

FURTHER READING

Paul L. Maier, *First Christmas* (New York: Harper & Row, 1971).

R. T. France, "Scripture, Tradition and History in the Infancy Narratives of Matthew," in *Gospel Perspectives,* ed. R. T. France and David Wenham, vol. 2 (Sheffield: JSOT Press, 1981).

11

MIRACLES AND THE
MODERN WORLD

Y ou might react to the title of this chapter by saying, "In the modern world we cannot be expected to believe that Jesus performed miracles." You may say, "People today know that the world is governed by the laws of nature, therefore miracles, or variations in those laws, simply cannot happen." "Since we don't see miracles nowadays," you may add, "the miracles in the New Testament must have arisen from the superstitious imagination of a prescientific age. Perhaps people at that time *thought* a miracle had taken place or *hoped* it had, but really they were mistaken."

The theologian will reply that it is Jesus, the central figure of the New Testament, who makes the difference. It is because God chose to "visit" our world in the person of his Son at that time and place that those extraordinary things happened in relationship to him. Understand that the great miracle is the incarnation of the Son of God, they argue, and the miracles are reasonable to believe. Indeed, if Jesus was "Emmanuel . . . God with us" (Mt 1:23) we should be surprised if miracles did not take place.

When we turn to the Gospels we find that the miracles of Jesus are pointed to as evidence of his true identity. Let us examine three sayings of Jesus that make this point.

The first is from the source known as Q, from which Matthew and Luke both quote:

If it is by the Spirit ["finger," Lk] of God that I cast out demons, then the kingdom of God has come upon you. (Mt 12:28 = Lk 11:20)

Jesus was the bearer of the kingdom or rule of God among them. In Jesus, God's will was being done on earth; God's kingdom had come. The miraculous exorcisms pointed to the presence of the kingdom in Jesus.

The second example is found in a passage in the Gospel of Mark where Jesus provocatively declares a paralyzed man's sins forgiven. When challenged that only God could forgive sins, Jesus declared:

> But that you may know that the Son of man has authority on earth to forgive sins . . . I say to you, rise, take up your pallet [bed] and go home. (Mk 2:10-11)

The miraculous healing of the man served to establish the shattering truth that Jesus, the Son of Man, bore the authority of God among men to forgive sins.

The third example is taken from the Gospel of John:

> If I am not doing the works of my Father, then do not believe me; but if I do them, even though you do not believe me, believe the works, that you may know and understand that the Father is in me and I am in the Father. (10:37-38; cf. 14:10-11)

If his hearers doubt what he says about himself, then let them look at what he does—what he calls "works of my Father." The miracle works of Jesus—giving sight to the blind and life to the dead—are the works of God his Father, full of compassion and divine power.

Jesus' contemporaries sensed that he possessed supernatural powers. There is good evidence (Mk 8:11; Mt 12:38-39) that they requested him to perform a heavenly sign, that is, to do something freakish or abnormal. Jesus' miracles of healing the sick or feeding the hungry (see Jn 6:30) were too mundane or ordinary to satisfy their craving for spectacular evidence.

The miracles of Jesus were restrained, always done for the good of those in need and not for show. Nevertheless, the effect of such actions was to indicate that the kingdom of God had come among them, that the Son of Man was present with them, authorized to forgive sins, and that the "Father was in him."

But are the miracles historical? Is there reasonable evidence for modern people to believe miracles took place? There are four reasons for confidence in the historicity of the miracles of Jesus.

First, there is evidence from the non-Christian sources, Josephus and the Talmud. Josephus, writing in the nineties, clearly intends us to understand that Jesus performed miracles when he states that "Jesus . . . wrought surprising feats" (*Antiquities* 18.63). The Talmud, written much later, says that "They hanged Yeshu" because "he practised sorcery" (*Sanhedrin* 43a) which is probably a reference to exorcism by the power of the devil, something Jesus was accused of in the Gospel account (Mk 3:22).

Second, the apostle Peter refers to the miracles of Jesus in his two major speeches as recorded in the Acts of the Apostles. On the day of Pentecost in the year 33 in Jerusalem Peter said:

> Jesus of Nazareth, a man attested to you by God with mighty works and wonders and signs which God did through him in your midst, as you yourselves know. (Acts 2:22)

Four or five years later, at the house of the centurion Cornelius in Caesarea, Peter stated:

> God anointed Jesus of Nazareth with the Holy Spirit and with power; how he went about doing good and healing all that were oppressed by the devil. (Acts 10:38)

Like the crowds in Jerusalem, Cornelius also knew of these remarkable deeds of Jesus (Acts 10:37). Peter's and Paul's speeches in Acts contain important historical information about Jesus. Paul makes no reference to Jesus' miracles, an omission that actually encourages our confidence in the authenticity of the speeches, since Paul was not an eyewitness to the historical Jesus.

Third, some scholars find the sayings of Jesus about miracles particularly significant, especially those that are readily translatable back into Aramaic, the language he spoke. Consider, for example, Jesus' reply to the messengers from John the Baptist:

> Tell John what you hear and see: the blind receive their sight and the lame walk, lepers are cleansed and the deaf hear, and the dead are raised up. (Mt 11:4-5)

Joachim Jeremias, an expert in Aramaic, argued that these words originally occurred in a speech rhythm which was characteristic of the way Jesus spoke.[1] In what is unquestionably an utterance of Jesus, appeal is made to what has been seen and heard in respect to miracles of healing the blind, the lame, the lepers, the deaf and raising the dead.

Again, in a passage common to Matthew and Luke, that is, belonging to the sayings source Q, Jesus said:

> Woe to you, Chorazin! woe to you, Bethsaida! for if the mighty works done in you had been done in Tyre and Sidon, they would have repented long ago. . . . And you, Capernaum . . . (Mt 11:21, 23; Lk 10:13, 15)

In a saying that is undoubtedly historical, Jesus appeals to miraculous events that, by common agreement, had happened in Chorazin, Bethsaida and Capernaum. This is powerful evidence for the historical truth of the miracles as Jeremias, who subjects the Scriptures to rigorous criticism, commented:

> Thus even when strict critical standards have been applied to the miracle stories, a demonstrably historical nucleus remains. Jesus performed healings that astonished his contemporaries.[2]

Fourth, there are many examples of multiple attestation to exorcism, nature miracles, healings and the raising of the dead in the primary Gospel sources Mark, John, Q, L and M, as the table on p. 109 clearly shows.[3]

MIRACLES IN THE GOSPEL SOURCES

It is important to note that the sources cited in the table arose independently of each other. Notice too that the whole range of miracle actions is attested. The breadth of attestation of the whole gamut of the miracles of Jesus is compelling historical evidence. Nature miracles, for example, are described in four of these five independent sources.

The evidence from non-Christian sources, from the Acts speeches, from the sayings of Jesus and from the primary Gospel strands combine to provide a solid basis for historical confidence in the miracles of Jesus. One might even say that this evidence is as good as, or better than, that for most other historical events or persons of that period.

	Mark	John	Q	L	M
Exorcism	Capernaum demoniac (1:21-28)			The dumb demoniac (9:32-34; cf. 10:5-8)	The dumb demoniac (9:32-34 cf 10:5-8)
	Gerasene demoniac (5:1-20)				
Nature Miracles	Stilling the storm (4:35-41)				
	Feeding the five thousand (6:30-44)	Feeding the five thousand (6:1-13)		Draft of fishes (5:1-11)	
	Walking on the water (6:45-52)	Walking on the water (6:16-21)			
Healing	Withered hand (3:1-6)	Official's son (4:46-54)	Centurion's boy (Mt 8:5-13)	Bent woman (13:10-17)	
	Blind Bartimaeus (10:46-52)	Man born blind (9:1-34)			
Resurrection	Daughter of Jairus (5:21-43)	Lazarus (11:1-44)		Widow's son (7:11-17)	

FURTHER READING

R. T. France, *The Man They Crucified* (Leicester, U.K.: Inter-Varsity Press, 1975).

Reginald Horace Fuller, *Interpreting the Miracles* (Philadelphia: Westminster Press, 1963).

Joachim Jeremias, *New Testament Theology,* trans. John Bowden, vol. 1 (London: SCM Press, 1971).

C. S. Lewis, *Miracles* (New York: Macmillan, 1978).

Géza Vermès, *Jesus the Jew* (Philadelphia: Fortress, 1981).

THE RESURRECTION
OF JESUS

The heart of the apostles' message was the resurrection of Jesus. Whether it was Peter preaching to Jews in Jerusalem or Paul preaching to Gentiles in Athens, their announcement focused on "the resurrection" of Jesus "from the dead" (Acts 4:33; 17:18). The focal point of the New Testament and of Christianity is, in Paul's words, "Jesus Christ, risen from the dead" (2 Tim 2:8).

The apostle Paul, then, was quite correct when he said:

> If Christ has not been raised, then our proclamation is in vain and your faith is in vain. We are even found to be misrepresenting God. (1 Cor 15:14)

Thus Christianity in a nutshell is (1) the proclamation by the apostles and (2) the faith of the church, that Christ was raised from the dead (cf. 1 Cor 15:11).

But if God did not, as a matter of fact, raise Jesus from the dead, then both proclamation and faith are vain (literally "empty"). Worst of all, these apostles, who were Jewish men, had proved to be "false witnesses" of the God of Israel.

In short, if the resurrection did not take place, the message and faith of Christianity were utterly devoid of reality and those who proclaimed it were blasphemers of their covenant God.

Historically, the raising of Jesus caused his identity claims as the Son of God to be validated and his sayings and actions remembered. There were a number of "messiahs" and "prophets" in that general era, each of them with followers. But, in each case, their movements died with them; almost nothing of their deeds or words has survived.

Jesus, however, was survived by an ongoing movement that went from strength to strength and quickly outgrew the following that had arisen during his ministry period. It was the fact of the resurrection and the coming of the Spirit that gave the impetus for this rapid growth.

In the period immediately after Jesus, the movement was bursting with activity. The Old Testament was scoured for possible references to the Christ who was to come. Lists of prophecies fulfilled in Jesus were gathered. Creeds and hymns focused on Jesus were written. A format to remember his death in the bread and the wine was created. His teaching was committed to memory and, in all probability, to written form (Lk 1:1). Ministry among Jews was exploding, which, in time, broke out of Jewish constraints in a number of semi-autonomous missions, including that of Philip to the Samaritans and God-fearers and Paul to the Gentiles.

It is highly unlikely that this whirl of activity would have occurred apart from the resurrection of Jesus. The resurrection is the eruption that set off the chain reaction within early Christianity: (1) in Jerusalem, the collection of now-fulfilled prophecies, the establishing of creedal and liturgical formulae, the writing of hymns to Jesus; (2) in Jerusalem and Judea the mission work among Jews; (3) the rapid spread of the mission to Samaria, Phoenicia, Cyprus, Syria; and (4) beyond that to Cilicia, Galatia, the provinces encircling the Aegean Sea and westward to Italy and to Rome itself.

It is apparent that the resurrection of Jesus from the dead is critical to Christianity. What evidence is there for its historical reality?

Many readers will not accept the God dimension, that is, the possibility of miracles and of supernatural intervention in time and space. For them, philosophically speaking, the resurrection is impossible. Perhaps, though, as the reader considers the historical evidence for the resurrection, the philosophical structure of thought will be enlarged. Based on evidence, if the resurrection did happen, then one's mindset about what might or might not happen has to be modified.

If we could spend a day in the shoes of first-century people, we would be confronted with a group of people who were convinced that their historical founder and leader had been raised from the dead.

Their follow-up literature in the Mission Letters assumes, but makes no effort to prove, the resurrection, so much is it taken to be beyond doubt. Key figures like James, Peter and Paul, who had nothing to do with one another before the first Easter, were each profoundly, though differently, changed by the fact of the resurrection. Separate but dovetailing traditions relating to the resurrection on the "first day of the week" and the "third day" after the crucifixion were in circulation, the one emanating from the Galilean women, the other from the twelve disciples. When the various accounts are compared, the risen Jesus was seen and heard by between five and six hundred people over twelve known occasions during a forty-day period. The life-and-death zeal these Jews had for Yahweh and for his temple and Sabbath was now expressed as life-and-death zeal for the risen Jesus, though the Sabbath was still observed and the temple attended.

REFERENCES TO RESURRECTION IN THE LETTERS ARE GRATUITOUS

When *gratuitous* is used in connection with movies or books, it refers to scenes involving violence or sex that are extraneous to the story line, meaning the story would not be affected if they were omitted.

The term may be applied to the New Testament because much of the information about the resurrection of Jesus is not part of the argument in a letter but is introduced gratuitously, to support that argument.

It is striking that the letters of the mission leaders—James, Peter, John and Paul—never argue for the truth of the resurrection of Jesus. The writers assume that the readers accept its reality as well established and not in contention.

This is not to say that the original hearers— whether they were Jews or Gentiles—would have accepted easily the resurrection of Jesus from the dead. Jews were looking for a universal resurrection at the end of history. The resurrection of an individual beforehand who was permanently—as opposed to temporarily—alive would have been a novelty. Gentiles of the Greek world believed in the immortality of the soul after the decay of the deceased. The resurrection of the body would have struck them as decidedly odd. Some of Paul's hearers in Athens, when they heard of the resurrection of the dead, mocked the apostle (Acts 17:32). Only powerful arguments from the apostles could have convinced Jews and Gentiles to become Christians and, in particular, to believe that Jesus was actually raised from the dead.

But this is not the situation we encounter in the Letters. Such references as there are to the resurrection are often made in passing, to reinforce some other aspect of Christian belief or behavior. Nonetheless, such references are frequent. To remove them would leave the New Testament an unreadable bundle of rags and tatters.

James and John do not make direct reference to the resurrection of Jesus. But they do speak of his second coming that, of course, is presupposed by his resurrection (Jas 5:9; 1 Jn 3:2). This indicates the degree to which both writers and readers took Jesus' resurrection to be an established fact.

Peter speaks of the resurrection of Jesus from the dead as the basis of the believers' faith and hope and of their forgiveness before God (1 Pet 1:3, 21; 3:18, 21). It is not something for which Peter has to contend but rather is given as a basis for godly confidence.

The gratuitous nature of resurrection references is illustrated by Paul's major reference to the resurrection of Jesus in 1 Corinthians 15:3-8. Paul is responding to a report that some of the Corinthians have expressed doubts about their own bodily resurrection. "How can some of you say there is no resurrection of the dead?" he asks (1 Cor 15:12). Paul corrects this theological error by appealing to the uncontroversial fact of the death, the burial, the resurrection on the third day and the subsequent appearances of the risen Christ on a number of occasions. The Corinthians will be raised from the dead because Christ *has been* raised from the dead (1 Cor 15:20-21). The fact is not in doubt and does not have to be argued. He is reminding them of something they already know as a basis of getting their thinking straight on this current issue.

We conclude that James, Peter, John and Paul—and with them Jude and the writer of Hebrews—were convinced of the truth of the resurrection of Jesus (Jude 21, Heb 1:3; 2:9; 13:20). Where did this conviction originate? There is no special pleading, no propping up of their case. The most reasonable explanation for their convictions is that they arose from fact, the fact that Jesus was raised from the dead.

THE OTHERWISE UNACCOUNTABLY CHANGED LIVES OF JAMES, PETER AND PAUL

Three of those named as having seen the risen Christ—James, Peter and Paul (1 Cor 15:3-8)—died as martyrs three decades after the resurrection. James was executed in Jerusalem A.D. 62 at the hands of the high priest Annas II, and Peter and Paul in Rome in the midsixties under the emperor Nero.

We are able to follow the life and movements of James and Peter over the previous thirty-five years and those of Paul over the previous thirty years. The records are extensive.

It is remarkable that these men, who became mission leaders as a result of the change the risen Christ made in their lives, apparently did not know one another beforehand. Nor were they agreed about all things as leaders of the various mission teams. Differences of opinion, even quarrels between them, are a matter of record (cf. Gal 2:11-14; 1 Cor 1:12; 9:5; Acts 21:18-21). But they were united in their belief in and proclamation of the resurrection of Jesus (1 Cor 15:5, 7-8, 11).

Critical questions are posed by the lives of these men. Why did James, Jesus' younger brother, who did not originally believe in Jesus (Jn 7:5), become his devoted servant after the first Easter? Why did Peter continue to serve Jesus after his death, having apparently expected the apocalyptic kingdom of God to intervene when Jesus arrived in Jerusalem? (See Lk 22:38, 49; 24:21; Jn 18:10; Acts 1:6.) Why did Paul begin to serve Jesus, having been a zealous persecutor of his followers (Gal 1:13-16)?

The resurrection of Jesus from the dead is critical to these questions. Peter would not have continued, nor James and Paul have begun, to serve Jesus unless these men were convinced that Jesus had been raised from the dead.

James had remained in Nazareth with his brothers and sisters and Mary after Jesus moved to Capernaum to commence his public ministry in Galilee. It is reasonable to suppose that he, too, had been a carpenter/builder like Joseph and his older brother. There is evidence of resentment, or even hostility, toward Jesus (Mk 3:21, 31-35). Yet, after the first Easter, James is found first as a member, then as the first of the three pillars, then as sole leader of the Jerusalem church (Acts 1:14; 12:17; Gal 1:19; 2:9; Acts 15:13; 21:18). James had been a totally unknown Nazarene. He became leader of a community of many thousands in Jerusalem. The Jewish historian Josephus describes his death at some length (*Jewish Antiquities* 20.200).

Peter changed from an obscure fisherman in the landlocked Sea of Galilee to a leader in an international movement. His travels took him from Galilee through Judea, Samaria, Phoenicia, Syria, Asia Minor and Greece to Italy, and the change takes some explaining.

Consider, too, the radical turnaround of *Saul,* the obsessive protector of the faith of his fathers who, as a leading activist, sought to destroy the heretical schism associated with Jesus. But this man became the leading promoter of that schism he had attempted to obliterate—and did so among the Gentiles, a people who, as a strict Pharisee, he would have despised for their idolatry and promiscuity. How can we account for this astonishing change? In his own words, it was because the Lord, who had been raised on the third day, appeared to him (1 Cor 15:8-9).

James, Peter and Saul/Paul each served the risen Lord for about thirty years—James in Judea, Peter and Paul on the world stage. It is difficult to believe that they would have done this unless they were convinced that Jesus was, indeed, the risen Lord. Is it possible to be so mistaken for *thirty* years? If they were liars, would they have suffered over so long a period, and then died for their lie? Their letters do not suggest either delusion or deceit, but clear thinking and burning integrity.

It might be argued that monks in eastern religions are prepared to die through self-immolation in the expectation of reincarnation, or that Islamic extremists will embrace suicide bombings for the bliss of Paradise. The leaders James, Peter and John, however, did not serve Christ and die for him in prospect of an unverifiable future life. Rather, they lived and died as they did on account of a verifiable historical event, the resurrection of Jesus. They did indeed die in the joyous prospect of reunion with Jesus. But it was a Jesus whom they knew had been raised from the dead because they had seen him alive.

In short, the lives and the deaths of James, Peter and Paul stand as monuments to the historicity of the resurrection of Jesus.

TWO SEPARATE TRADITIONS: THE "THIRD DAY" AND THE "FIRST DAY"

There are two strands of information that are different in detail but not contradictory to the central fact of the resurrection. One is the tradition, quoted by Paul, that Jesus was "raised on the *third* day" (1 Cor 15:3). The other, found in each of the four Gospels, states that the women came to the tomb in which Jesus was buried on the *"first* day of the week" and found it empty; the body of Jesus was not there.

Both traditions mention a day. The one pinpoints the resurrection day counted from the death of Jesus, the other to its occurrence in the course of the week.

Tradition 1: Jesus was "raised on the third day." In the midfifties Paul wrote reminding the Corinthians of the statement they had "received" from him five years earlier

that [Christ] was raised on the third day in accordance with the scriptures. (1 Cor 15:4; cf. Acts 10:40)

But Paul did not compose this statement. He too had "received" it as a preformed piece of information in the midthirties. Since the first Easter occurred in 33, this confession must have been formulated in the two- to three-year period between that first Easter and Paul's first visit as a Christian to Jerusalem (Gal 1:18-19).

Jesus died and was buried late on the Friday afternoon: day one (part days were then counted as full days). The second day, the Sabbath, began—by Jewish reckoning—at sunset on Friday and lasted until sunset on Saturday. The third day was from sunset Saturday to sunset Sunday. It was within this "third day" that Jesus "was raised" from the dead.

The "third day" as a detail ties down the precise twenty-four-hour period in which Jesus was raised. It was incorporated into this, the earliest creed of Christianity, which Paul "received" and which, in turn, he "handed over" to the Corinthians. Thus the "third day" immediately became part of the pattern of the apostolic preaching of the gospel of Christ.

That this tradition emanated from the Jerusalem leadership to Paul is corroborated by its place in Peter's proclamation of the gospel (Acts 10:40). In

the next century the "third day" is found in the earliest forms of the Apostles'
Creed. Clearly the "third day" tradition was widely proclaimed and confessed from the beginning.

Tradition 2: Raised the "first day." Each of the four Gospels indicates
that early in the morning of the "first day of the week"—Sunday—the
women who returned to the tomb found it empty; the body of Jesus was not
there. (See Mt 28:1-6; Mk 16:1-6; Lk 24:1-3; Jn 20:13.)

Nor were the women alone in witnessing the empty tomb. Luke and John
record that several of the disciples, upon hearing the report of the women,
came to the tomb and found only grave cloths. Among these witnesses is
John, the author of the Fourth Gospel (Jn 20:2-8; 21:24).

Jesus had died midafternoon Friday. The Sabbath was rapidly approach-
ing, after which no work—such as burying a corpse—could be done. Moreover, to leave a corpse hanging at Passover Sabbath would have brought defilement to the land (Deut 21:23; cf. Jn 19:31-32).

Joseph, a member of the Sanhedrin who was a secret follower of Jesus,
resolved the problem. He sought and received permission from the Romans
to take the body down from the cross and to bury it. Joseph owned a rock
tomb near Golgotha, the site of the crucifixion (Mt 27:60).

The faithful women from Galilee, who had witnessed the death of Jesus
and his interment in the tomb, decided to return as soon as possible to
anoint and spice the body. Early on the Sunday morning—the first day of
the week—afforded the first real opportunity to do this.

But the body was gone.

The Gospel writer makes a point of saying that the disciples were "again
in the house" eight days later, that is, on the following Sunday. It seems to
be established that from that time the disciples of the Lord Jesus gathered on
"the first day of the week," the "Lord's Day" (Acts 20:7; 1 Cor 16:2; Rev
1:10). Thus from the very next Sunday after the tomb was found empty until
today Christians have met together on Sunday as the church of Jesus, in recognition that God raised him from the dead on that day. The Sunday gath-
ering, therefore, is like a monument to the resurrection of the Lord.

The "first day" tradition almost certainly rests on the recollection of the
women who came to the tomb in which Jesus had been buried. The "third

day" tradition was probably influenced by Jesus' repeated prophecy that he would be raised "after three days." We might have expected the Gospels to narrate the discovery of the empty tomb on the "third day," in line with so much Jesus said about the "third day" in the Gospels. (See Jn 2:19; cf. Mk 14:58; Lk 13:31-35; Mt 12:40-41; Mk 8:31; 9:31; 10:34.) But to our surprise it is the "first day of the week" that they come to the tomb, which, because it comes so unexpectedly, enhances the credibility of the account. It is the testimony of the women that the resurrection occurred on "the first day" that informs the four Gospels.

Jesus' words about "three days" came to be included within the church's first creed, which was formulated at Jerusalem where Paul "received" it (1 Cor 15:4; cf. Acts 10:40). Peter, the disciple of Jesus who had often heard the Lord speak about the "third day," was almost certainly the source of the "third day" tradition to Paul (1 Cor 15:4; Gal 1:18-19), a tradition that he himself uses in his own gospel preaching (Acts 10:40).

The two traditions, which arose separately—the one from the women, the other from the disciples—combine powerfully to reinforce the reality of the resurrection. The one, originating from the women's experience, pinpoints the day of the week when the tomb was found to be empty. The other, arising from the apostles' public proclamation (cf. Acts 10:40), which in turn was dependent on Jesus' prophecies, establishes which day it was relative to Jesus' death that Jesus was raised from the dead.

To this day Christians endorse the reality of the resurrection by two practices that go back to the very beginnings of the resurrection church. One is that they meet on the "first day of the week," the "Lord's day." The other is that in the creed they confess, they declare that it was on the "third day" that God raised his Son from the dead.

ALTERNATIVE EXPLANATIONS

A number of alternative explanations have been offered to the testimony of the New Testament, that Jesus was raised from the dead.

The resurrection was a hoax. There have been many spectacular hoaxes in history. Some remained unexploded for considerable periods. It was not until 1953 that Charles Dawson's 1912 "Piltdown Man" finally was revealed to be the remains of a very modern ape. In 1994 it was shown that the 1930s photo of the head of the Loch Ness "monster," which became known worldwide, was actually a contraption made for the purpose of deception.

Was the greatest hoax of all, however, the story of the resurrection of Jesus of Nazareth? It is a story that has been believed by millions throughout the two millennia since.

Hoaxes are hard to conceal indefinitely, the more so if more than one or two perpetrators are involved, as there would have been in this case. The truth has a way of floating to the surface sooner or later. The Shroud of Turin now stands exposed for what it was, a medieval hoax.

Hoaxes also need the right soil and climate to take root and flourish. "Piltdown Man" was credible enough in an era of eager interest in anthropological origins. The brooding waters of the great Scottish Loch make a "monster" believable, and it will take more than disclosures of a photographic hoax to overturn the faith of many in "Nessie."

But the resurrection of Jesus was, as it were, against the run of play. Jews were then expecting resurrection, but it would happen at the *end* of history and it would involve *every* person who had ever died. Thomas's skepticism about resurrection reports was probably a typical reaction. To assert that *one* person had been raised permanently *that* day would be as unimaginable and unacceptable as announcing to World Cup soccer fans at halftime that the game was over and that there would be no second half.

To Greeks of the period, who believed in a soul's immortality, the declaration that the man Jesus had been resurrected was quite laughable (Acts 17:32). The times and circumstances of "Piltdown Man" and "Nessie" facilitated believability, but so far as Jews and Greeks of the period were concerned, the resurrection of Jesus came straight out of left field.

Perhaps, then, the biblical story arose from an urban myth? Did it originate somehow like the story about the man with dreadlocks who died, bitten by the Red Back spiders that had nested in his amazing hair?

The thing about urban myths is that you can never track them to their source. When did it happen? In which hospital? What was the man's name? The story just disappears into the fog. But it was not like that with Jesus. We know who owned the tomb where he was buried on the Friday but from which the body was missing at first light on Sunday. Nor was the owner a nonentity; he was an eminent citizen of Jerusalem, Joseph from Arimathea, a member of the Supreme Council. No problem tracking him down and getting the facts. The emptiness of that tomb must be regarded as one of the most secure facts of the ancient world. That Matthew must disprove the current rebuttal of its emptiness is evidence of that (Mt 28:11-15).

We also know when, where and to whom the risen Jesus presented himself. Embedded in history a mere twenty years after the event, Paul states that more than five hundred saw him on one occasion, most of whom are alive at the time of Paul's writing (1 Cor 15:6). In Jerusalem and Galilee he was seen alive by Mary Magdalene and the other named women from Galilee and by the disciples whose names we know throughout a forty-day period and by Saul some months later. The remarkable story is readily traceable at many points. This is not the stuff of urban myths.

Another man was crucified. The Qur'an holds that Jesus was a prophet and that, since God would not allow his prophet to be treated that way, another man was crucified in Jesus' place. It states, "They did not kill [Jesus] nor did they crucify him but they thought they did. . . . It was sheer conjecture" (Sura 4:156).

This goes against all the evidence. It was precisely because Jesus was a public figure in Jerusalem that the temple authorities and the Romans wanted him out of the way. Hundreds of thousands of Jewish pilgrims congregated in Jerusalem at Passover time. Past events had shown that the tiniest spark could ignite riot and tumult in such a volatile situation.

Although Jesus was arrested at night, tried before a hastily convened Sanhedrin and then brought to Pilate in the early hours of the morning, the execution was very public. Jesus, along with two revolutionary activists, was crucified close to the walls of Jerusalem, near a well-used thoroughfare (Jn 19:20; Mk 15:29). The very point of crucifixion was to humiliate the felon *publicly* so as to deter others from such rash behavior.

There is every indication that it was Jesus who was crucified. Those who mocked him identified him as he hung on the cross: "He saved others" (Mk 15:31). Roman soldiers were present guarding the crucified men. Soon afterward Peter appeals to the people gathered in Jerusalem in regard to Jesus, who had been well-known to them: "*This Jesus,* whom you crucified . . . *this Jesus* God raised up" (Acts 2:36, 32).

It was Jesus who was crucified, not another.

Jesus did not actually die on the cross. The "swoon" theory, as it is called, was argued in the early 1800s by German scholars Venturini and Paulus, and more recently by the British academic J. Duncan Derrett.[1] Jesus became unconscious on the cross but revived in the tomb.

This theory is made in ignorance of the Roman practice of crucifixion. The Jewish historian Josephus records many instances of Roman crucifixion in Palestine. Not only was crucifixion itself violent in the extreme, it was preceded and accompanied by brutal torture. Roman soldiers took full advantage of the utter vulnerability of the victims. Sadism reigned supreme before and during crucifixion. Taken together, the scourging and the nailing up of the victim represented an overwhelming assault on the human frame that left the person critically debilitated. Those not already dead died upon removal from the cross.

Religious art has given a false impression of the man on the cross as motionless and quietly dignified. But it would have been otherwise.

Death came by asphyxiation. The downward weight of the body constricted breathing, so that the impaled person constantly sought to writhe upward to expand the lungs. The crucified used their feet and their legs to lever themselves up so as to breathe. If, however, the executioners broke the legs, the victims had no leverage and thus could not breathe; death came quickly.

This is precisely what the Roman soldiers began to do late on that Friday afternoon. Bodies left impaled on the Sabbath during Passover brought defilement to the land. When the Jews requested that the three men be killed so as to permit burial before the onset of the Sabbath, the Roman soldiers began to break the legs of the victims. When they came to Jesus, however, they found that he was already dead.

One of the execution squad thrust a spear into Jesus to gauge whether he was in fact dead, as he appeared to be. The sudden flow of blood and water was taken to be evidence of the reality of the death. Although the dead do not bleed, the blood often remains liquid in the arteries for some hours following asphyxial deaths. Depending on the organs or the blood vessels pierced, for example the inferior vena cava, water and serum could indeed issue from someone recently deceased, especially if crucified vertically. The Roman soldiers were trained and experienced at their grim work.

John, author of the Fourth Gospel, was present when Jesus breathed his last breath. He gives eyewitness testimony that Jesus was truly dead (Jn 21:24; 19:35).

The body of Jesus remained on the cross until the centurion of the execution squad had come to the prefect, Pontius Pilate, and convinced him that Jesus was dead (Mk 15:34-35). The prefect only released the body for burial upon the centurion's assurances that Jesus was indeed dead. This was no mere formality in the case of Jesus. The brevity of the time Jesus had been crucified led the prefect to press the question whether or not he was dead. But the answers of the centurion convinced him.

All the evidence agrees that Jesus died that afternoon.

The body was removed from the tomb. The reason the tomb was empty—it is claimed—is that someone removed the corpse between the time of the burial late on Friday afternoon and the arrival of the women early on Sunday morning.

Who might have done this and why?

Neither Jews nor Romans would have wanted the body to be anyplace other than in the tomb, as powerful evidence that the influential malefactor was indeed dead. Such was to be the fate of those who create public disturbance! Both Jews and Romans could point to the place where he was crucified and the place where he was buried. The bones of Jesus in the tomb in which he was buried would stand as irrefutable denial of the claims he had made and the hopes that had been invested in him.

In any case, had either Jew or Roman taken the body, they would have immediately produced it when the disciples began to proclaim that Jesus had risen.

It was widely believed at the time that the *disciples* had taken the body. But Matthew states that the temple authorities bribed the Roman soldiers to say this (Mt 28:11-15). Matthew's rebuttal of the widespread belief among the Jews that the disciples had taken the body is very clear evidence that the tomb in which Jesus had been buried did not contain his body. Indeed, throughout the next two centuries the Jewish counterclaims continued that the disciples had taken the body.[2]

This, however, is entirely improbable. The disciples had not understood Jesus' earlier words about being raised after three days (Mk 9:10). As Jews they believed (1) in the *universal* resurrection of everyone who had ever died that (2) will occur at the *end* of history. Martha told Jesus that her brother would rise again in *the* resurrection in *the last day* (Jn 11:24). This was Jewish orthodoxy, to which the disciples would have subscribed. An *individual's* permanent resurrection, now—*before* the end of history—would have been unimaginable, quite outside their well-established frame of reference.

The disciples had come armed to Jerusalem (Lk 22:49-50; Jn 19:10; cf. Lk 19:11) expecting a messianic showdown (Acts 1:6; cf. Lk 24:21). They did not expect Jesus to be raised, because they did not expect him to be killed. By definition the Messiah was a victor and they had come with him to share in the spoils of his apocalyptic triumph. On the way to Jerusalem, James and John wanted to have places of power when he entered into his glory (Mk 10:35-37). Jesus' words about his death and resurrection as they traveled to Jerusalem fell on deaf ears (Mk 9:10; 10:32). The disciples greeted with disbelief the women's report that the tomb was empty and that Jesus' promise that he would be raised on the third day had been fulfilled (Lk 24:11).

The suggestion, then, that these deeply disappointed men, steeped in an apocalyptic worldview, suddenly thought of stealing the body and saying that Jesus, as an individual, had been raised from the dead before the onset of the end of the world is extremely improbable.

The women returned to the wrong tomb. This explanation states that the women made the simplest mistake: they returned to the wrong tomb, found it empty and declared that the Lord had risen.[3]

By the time Jesus had died it was middle-late afternoon; a new day, the Sabbath, would soon begin. With the rapid onset of the Passover Sabbath Jesus must be taken from the cross and interred, otherwise the land would be defiled (Deut 21:23; Jn 19:31, 42).

The records show that Joseph of Arimathea, a member of the Sanhedrin, made his as-yet-unused tomb available for the burial of Jesus (Mt 27:60). It is clear from the records that Joseph's tomb was close to Golgotha, the site of the crucifixion (Jn 19:40, 42). Golgotha itself was close to the walls of Jerusalem; the *titulus*, or caption attached to Jesus' cross, could be read from the city wall (Jn 19:20). In other words, the tomb was readily locatable, being (1) close to Jesus' cross that was close to the city walls and (2) doubtless a substantial tomb, belonging to one of the most prominent members of the community.

Each Gospel tells us that the tomb to which the women came and found to be empty belonged to a man of high profile with whom the story could be readily checked. Moreover, the Gospels indicate that the women sat opposite the tomb; they saw "where" and "how" the burial occurred (Mt 27:61; Mk 15:47; Lk 23:55). The "mistaken tomb" explanation is improbable and goes against the evidence given for the burial of Jesus.

But disciples also came to the tomb on the report of the women (Lk 24:24). John, author of the Fourth Gospel, was one of those who came to the tomb. He testifies as an eyewitness that only Jesus' burial cloths were in the tomb (Jn 20:5-8). The presence of burial cloths confirms that the women had indeed come to the right place. Clearly they had come to the tomb in which Jesus had been buried.

The resurrection stories are legends. It is well established that legends take many years—in fact decades and centuries—to develop.

But the "first day of the week" tradition arises from the women who went to the tomb. It became fixed immediately as the significant day of the week, because from the beginning the disciples began to meet on that day, the "first day of the week," to commemorate the Lord's resurrection (Jn 20:26; cf. Acts 20:7; 1 Cor 16:2).

The "third day" tradition can also be fixed in time. It was well established by the midthirties when Paul "received" it from the hands of the leaders of the Jerusalem church.

This is not the stuff of legends, but of history. These markers—"first day of the week" and "on the third day"—arose immediately after and for no other reason than the event of the resurrection of Jesus.

The resurrection originated in the Osiris myth. Some people argue that the Egyptian myth of Isis and Osiris is the real source of the New Testament proclamation of the resurrection of Jesus. The ancient Egyptian myth of Isis and Osiris, in a Hellenized form, became a widely followed cult around the Mediterranean world in the centuries after Alexander's conquest of Egypt in the fourth century before Christ.

According to the myth, Osiris, who had been a pharaoh, was murdered and mutilated by his brother Set. Isis, Osiris's sister and wife, collected and buried his remains and caused him to be reanimated as the god of the dead. Thus Osiris reigns over the underworld as a mummy; his "new life" is a replica of earthly life.

The association of Jesus with Osiris was fashionable in earlier generations, largely through the influence of James Frazer's *The Golden Bough*, published in 1906. The German scholar Rudolph Bultmann advocated a version of the dying and rising god as the explanation of the resurrection of Jesus. Bultmann's supposed parallels, however, all postdate the New Testament by several hundred years. Few today pursue this line of thought.

We should note that (1) the grotesque story of Isis and Osiris is quite unlike the account of the resurrection of Jesus; (2) as devout Jews, and therefore monotheists, the disciples would have had no part in an idolatrous Gentile cult or its beliefs; (3) the account about Jesus gives people, time and place—specifics that are not found in myths, which are ahistorical; (4) the formal credo about the resurrection of Jesus had been established within so brief a period as two or three years of the event; and (5) Jesus is not a reanimated god over the netherworld; rather, he is alive for evermore, the Lord of both the dead and the living (Rev 1:18; Rom 14:9).

JESUS APPEARED ALIVE FROM THE DEAD ON MANY OCCASIONS

According to the Acts of the Apostles, Jesus, after his sufferings, "presented himself alive . . . by many proofs, appearing to them during forty days" (Acts 1:3).

Within the New Testament there are five narratives of the appearances of the risen Jesus, Paul's and the four Gospel writers'.

Paul. The first letter to the Corinthians can be dated at A.D. 55 and probably predates the writing of the Gospels. Paul's words in 1 Corinthians 15:3-8, however, are not his own. He is quoting a preformed set of statements about Christ that he "received," almost certainly in the midthirties from the hands of the leaders of the Jerusalem church (Gal 1:18-19; cf. 2:8-9). These statements, therefore, are very close to Jesus and were formulated within two years of the first Easter.

> What I . . . received,
> that Christ died for our sins in accordance with the scriptures,
> that he was buried,
> that he was raised on the third day in accordance with
>   the scriptures, . . .
> that he appeared to Cephas,
> then to the twelve.
> Then he appeared to more than five hundred brethren at one time,
> most of whom are still alive, though some have fallen asleep.
> Then he appeared to James,
> then to all the apostles.
> Last of all . . . he appeared also to me.

Paul's "what" signifies something objective, an entity, and a raft of four facts.[4] This "what" is expanded on by four statements each introduced by "that." Each "that" (Greek *hoti*) signifies a separate statement in quotation marks (Greek language then lacked punctuation marks).

But the four statements are logically interconnected: Christ died *and* was buried *and* was raised on the third day *and* appeared to various people. The four statements are of a piece; they form one complete statement about what happened to Christ at the time of the first Easter. He died, was buried, was raised and appeared.

Each statement depends on its predecessor: Christ appeared *because* he had been raised; he was raised because he had been buried; he was buried because he had died. Having died, Christ was *entombed*.[5]

He was *raised* on the *third* day. Paul's Greek here betrays an underlying Aramaic form of words, literally "Christ . . . was raised in the day the third." The uncorrected Greek echoes the confession of the Aramaic-speaking community in Jerusalem from whom Paul received it.

He appeared on six occasions, the "then . . . then . . . then . . . then . . . last of all," suggesting due sequence. The first two probably occurred in Jerusalem, the third and fourth in Galilee, the fifth in Jerusalem and the sixth—to Saul—near Damascus.

The names of those to whom he appeared—and who saw him—are either given (Cephas = Peter, the Twelve, James, Paul) or may readily be ascertained (the five hundred, all the apostles). The witnesses to this event can be interrogated, including the vast number of five hundred who saw the risen Christ on one occasion. The sources of this remarkable event are identified and accessible. Let those who doubt go and enquire of these people themselves.

There is nothing vague here. The language is specific. Paul's is a statement of remarkable precision. It gives the lie to various "explanations"—which are really rationalizations—like the "swoon" theory, the "wrong tomb" theory, the "mistaken identity" theory or the "stolen body" theory.

John. John, the author of the Fourth Gospel, claims, like Paul, to have seen the risen Christ. He testifies to having seen Jesus die, to have come to the empty tomb where he saw the burial cloths and to have seen the risen Lord.

Of the four Gospel writers, this writer devotes the greatest space to the resurrection appearances of Jesus (fifty-six verses). The risen Jesus appeared to Mary Magdalene on the first day of the week (Sunday). Later that day he appeared to the disciples, Thomas being absent. Eight days later, the next Sunday by inclusive counting, he appeared again to the disciples, Thomas now being present. On one other occasion—noted as the third to his disciples—Jesus appeared in Galilee, by the Sea of Tiberias, to seven of his disciples, five of whom are named.

However, John is not writing primarily to convince his readers about the truth of the resurrection, but more particularly to establish the character of Jesus' resurrection body. As raised from the dead, Jesus had a physical body, but it was not limited in its movements. Nor was Jesus destined to remain here. He must go to his Father in order that another "comforter," the Holy Spirit, may come. True as it is that Thomas's doubt is exposed to show that there can be no doubt, John also writes to underline the importance of faith based on the word rather than on sight. Furthermore, John also wishes to highlight Peter's special future role in feeding Christ's sheep. John writes to establish these things rather than narrate or prove the resurrection of Jesus.

Luke. Luke gives the next greatest volume of information about Jesus' resurrection appearances (fifty-two verses). Luke (1) notes that Jesus had appeared to Peter, (2) narrates at length his conversation with Cleopas and another man walking to Emmaus, (3) recounts Jesus' meeting with the Eleven in Jerusalem as well as (4) his final contact with them at Bethany.

As with John, Luke is not attempting to establish the fact of the resurrection. That he assumes. Rather, Luke is narrating the appearances of Jesus so as to teach about the nature of Jesus' resurrected person. On one hand Jesus is risen as a physical body (he eats, drinks, shows his wounds); on the other, he is not now limited by physical constraints. Luke is preparing his readers for Jesus' eventual absence, when he will not be present with them. This he records in his second volume, the Acts of the Apostles.

Nonetheless, though it may not have been his primary intention, Luke's account, like John's, serves powerfully to establish the fact of the resurrection.

Matthew. Matthew records two appearances of the risen Jesus—one to the faithful Galilean women in Jerusalem, the other to the eleven disciples in Galilee.

Matthew assumes, rather than seeks to prove, the fact of the resurrection. His point instead is to show that Jesus is to be worshiped as the One who has all authority and that the message about him is to be taken to the nations. It will be remembered that he is introduced in the opening chapters as the Christ who as a child is worshiped by representatives from the nations, the magi. The resurrection appearances, in both of which Jesus is worshiped, form a fitting conclusion and climax to the entire Gospel of Matthew.

Mark. Mark gives no account of a resurrection appearance. Nonetheless, it is clear that the disciples in Galilee will see him. The tomb is empty. Jesus is not where he was buried; he is risen.

Mark is not intent on proving the fact of the resurrection. As with the other Gospel writers, this is something he assumes. Rather, Mark is seeking to rivet our attention on the future and final appearance of Jesus. His dramatic account of the emptiness of the tomb, the absence of Jesus and the awestruck fear of the women that dominate the final sentences of the Gospel take the reader to the edge of the eschatological abyss. We will not see Jesus again until his return. To recount resurrection appearances would have been a distraction so far as Mark's purposes are concerned.

Summary: resurrection appearances. There are five narratives of Jesus' resurrection appearances. Yet none of them sets out—as its primary intention—to prove the fact of the resurrection. Paul merely repeats what the Corinthians already believe to demonstrate the inconsistency of doubting the resurrection of *their* bodies. Each Gospel writer has his own point to make as he narrates these appearances or even, in Mark's case, Jesus' non-appearance.

In each narrative, names are given of those to whom the risen Christ presented himself. Astonishing as the story of Jesus' resurrection is, it is no urban myth, which by its nature disappears into the fog leaving the story unverifiable. Let the reader understand that the sources can be traced and checked.

From these five accounts we can list twelve known separate occasions when the risen Christ appeared to individuals or groups. This is the more impressive when it is noted that these narratives arise from separate and independent traditions.

Number of Appearances	1 Corinthians 15	John 20—21	Luke 24	Matthew 28
1		Mary (20:15)		
2				women (v. 6)
3	[Christ] appeared to Cephas (v. 5)		Simon (v. 34)	
4			2 men (v. 15)	
5	next to the Twelve (v. 5)	[1] disciples (20:17)	disciples (v. 36)	
6		[2] disciples (20:26)		
7		[3] 7 disciples (21:1)		
8	next to 500+ (v. 6)			
9				disciples in Galilee (v. 16)
10	next to James (v. 7)			
11	next to all the apostles (v. 7)		disciples (v. 50)	
12	last of all Paul (v. 8)			

While there is some uncertainty as to the precise sequence, we may say that the risen Christ appeared to our knowledge on twelve separate occasions, to both individuals and to groups. He was seen, heard and touched at different times and places. The names of those to whom he appeared are either given or at least are readily ascertainable.

There is some difficulty harmonizing the accounts of the resurrection appearances as recorded in our sources, something that has been pointed to as evidence of unreliability.[6] It should be pointed out, however, that neither Paul nor the Gospel writers are setting out to prove or even to systematically narrate the history of Jesus' resurrection appearances. These authors write from the assumption that their readers know about and believe the resurrection took place. Furthermore, the very existence of loose ends is evidence that these writers have not contrived a harmonious, even account. The discrepancies are a reason to believe in the naive integrity of the writers and indeed are not unusual in writers of the period. Three historians who narrate the Great Fire of Rome in A.D. 64 disagree about Nero's whereabouts during the fire and whether he "fiddled" (played the lyre) or sang while the city burned. But no one doubts that Nero failed to show leadership while the city was being destroyed.

In short, Jesus' resurrection appearances to so many people and at different times and places as recorded by Paul and the Gospel writers argues powerfully for the truth of the resurrection. Remarkably, the information is given gratuitously, almost casually, as if its incontrovertible nature is axiomatic. In each case the writer was seeking to go beyond the fact of the resurrection to make another point.

ALTERNATIVES TO THE RESURRECTION OF JESUS AS PHYSICAL

It is quite clear that something left its mark on history in early April, A.D. 33. Some who find the notion of Jesus' bodily resurrection unacceptable opt for another alternative, either (1) that the disciples saw Jesus in some kind of visionary sense,[7] or (2) that Jesus' body was *spiritual*, not physical, or (3) that the disciples underwent a "resurrection" as they reflected further on Jesus' death in the weeks after the event.

In regard to the first alternative mentioned, Jesus appeared to both individuals and groups in various places over a forty-day period. They ate with him and touched him. They heard as well as saw him. The risen Jesus did not exist in their minds but was encountered objectively and physically, external to them.

From the psychological viewpoint this first explanation runs contrary to the situation as it was that Passover. The disciples had expected a messianic coup, a divine intervention to bring in the kingdom of God (Lk 24:19-21). The arrest and execution of their leader left them demoralized and afraid at first to go out of doors (Jn 20:19). They greeted the news of Jesus' resurrection as stupid (Lk 24:11). They were not, in fact, psychologically conditioned for this supposed vision or hallucination.

The New Testament knows the difference between seeing the risen Lord and seeing a vision of the Lord. There are a number of visions of the Lord referred to in the New Testament, for example, by Stephen and by Paul (Acts 7:56; 18:9). But what these people saw during these forty days, and Paul after that, was no vision but the objectively risen person, Jesus.

Some scholars advocate the second notion on the basis of Paul's words in 1 Corinthians that because the body is raised as a *spiritual* body, and flesh and blood cannot inherit the kingdom of God (1 Cor 15:44, 50), Christ must have been raised as a *spiritual*, nonphysical body.

But in the passage in question (1 Cor 15:35-58), Paul is not discussing Christ's resurrection body but the believers' resurrection body. As uniquely filled with the Spirit of God, Jesus was the embodiment on earth of the kingdom of God. Humans need to be transformed for the kingdom of God; Jesus Christ did not.

In any case, Paul's contrast is not between a physical and a spiritual body but between the human, this-worldly or "natural" (*psychikos*) body and the supernatural or spiritual (*pneumatikos*) body. The former body is for this age, "natural," unregenerate (see 1 Cor 2:14); the latter—which is now Spirit-dominated—is for the coming age.

The third view—that the disciples had a kind of spiritual resurrection in the aftermath of the crucifixion as they came to see Jesus "alive"—has been advanced by Bishop John Shelby Spong.[8] Spong holds that there was no empty tomb because Jesus was thrown into a common grave, and there were no appearances because the corpse remained dead. Rather, Spong states, once back in Galilee Peter, reflecting on the crucifixion, underwent a "resurrection," believing that Jesus was now "alive." It was Peter, not Jesus, who was "resurrected." One wonders, how is Spong's view different from those who believe somehow that Elvis "still lives"?

Spong holds that Jesus was exalted directly from the grave to the right hand of God so that Paul and the other witnesses cited by him (1 Cor 15:3-8) did not see the Jesus who was resurrected from the grave but a heavenly vision, a revelation. But the apostles preached "the resurrection *of the dead*," not a spiritual exaltation of Jesus "from the grave to the right hand of God."

Spong's view that Jesus' body remained in the grave is at odds with the testimony of the apostles Peter and Paul, whose missionary speeches are quoted in the Acts of the Apostles in chapters 2 and 13 (see Acts 2:23-32; 13:29-37). Both apostles insist that Jesus was buried in a tomb, but that—in fulfillment of Psalm 16—the flesh of God's Holy One did not see corruption. Rather, God raised him *physically* from the dead.

David, the author of that psalm, is indeed dead. The location of David's tomb, which contained his mortal remains, was still known (and venerated?) at that time. But Jesus, the Holy One whose coming David had prophesied, did not see corruption. David saw corruption following his death, but Jesus, whom he prophesied, did not. On the contrary, Jesus appeared alive from the dead to those who had accompanied him from Galilee, who now bear witness to his resurrection from the dead. In quoting Psalm 16, both apostles make it crystal clear that Jesus was raised physically from the dead.

CONCLUSION

The analysis of the resurrection belongs to disciplines that evaluate evidence, in particular those of the historian and the lawyer.

An eminent historian of the period, Paul L. Maier, with due care, gave this opinion:

> If all the evidence is weighed carefully and fairly, it is indeed justifiable, according to the canons of historical research, to conclude that the tomb in which Jesus was buried was actually empty on the morn-

ing of the First Easter. And no shred of evidence has yet been discovered in literary sources, epigraphy or archaeology that would disprove this statement.[9]

The discipline of legal prosecution closely resembles that of the historian. Both must weigh and evaluate evidence as a basis for arriving at a reasonable conclusion. A noted jurist, Sir Edward Clarke, commented:

> The evidence for [the events of the first Easter Day] is conclusive, and over and over again in the High Court I have secured the verdict on evidence not nearly so compelling. . . . A truthful witness is always artless and disdains effect. The Gospel evidence for the resurrection is of this class and, as a lawyer, I accept it unreservedly as the testimony of truthful men to facts they were able to substantiate.[10]

Finally, we quote the well-known question of Professor C. F. D. Moule of Cambridge:

> If the coming into existence of the Nazarenes . . . rips a great hole in history, a hole the size and shape of the Resurrection, what does the secular historian propose to stop it up with?[11]

Let the reader honestly face the evidence for the resurrection and reach his or her own conclusions. Reduced to basics the alternatives are either (1) that one has to accept the evidence as true or (2) to conclude that an elaborate fraud has been perpetrated on the human race. For me, the quality of the evidence and the moral tone of the literature in which it occurs lead me to conclude that Jesus, having been killed was, after three days, raised from the dead on the first day of Passover week.

FURTHER READING

K. Baker, "The Resurrection of Jesus in Its Graeco-Roman Setting," *Reformed Theological Review* 62 (2003): 1-3.

Paul Copan, *Will the Real Jesus Please Stand Up?* (Grand Rapids: Baker, 1998).

William Lane Craig, *Apologetics* (Chicago: Moody Press, 1984).

———, "The Empty Tomb of Jesus," in *Gospel Perspectives*, ed. R. T. France and David Wenham, vol. 2 (Sheffield: JSOT, 1981).

Murray J. Harris, *Raised Immortal* (Grand Rapids: Eerdmans, 1985).

———, *Three Crucial Questions* (Grand Rapids: Eerdmans, 1994).

George Eldon Ladd, *I Believe in the Resurrection of Jesus* (Grand Rapids: Eerdmans, 1975).

Kategoria 15 (1999) with articles by Ken Handley, Peter Bolt and E. A. Judge.

N. T. Wright, *The Resurrection of the Son of God* (Minneapolis: Fortress, 2003).

PAUL AND THE HISTORICAL JESUS

Paul wrote his letters within the period A.D. 50-65(?).[1] So far as we know, the written Gospels were not in existence when he began writing. What can we learn from Paul about the historical Jesus? How much would we know about Jesus if the Gospels did not exist and we were solely dependent on Paul?

REVELATION AND TRADITION

Paul's knowledge of Jesus can be summed up in two Greek words: *apokalypsis* and *paradosis*. The first word is related to the verb "to veil" *(kalyptein)*. When *apo* is prefixed it means "*un*veil" or "reveal." Thus the noun *apokalypsis* signifies "unveiling" or "revelation." Paul wrote to the Galatians:

> The gospel which was preached by me is not man's gospel. . . . It came through a revelation of Jesus Christ. (Gal 1:11-12)

It was on the road near Damascus that God "was pleased to reveal his Son" to him (Gal 1:16). Paul's life as a Christian and also as an apostle began at the moment of that remarkable event. Moreover, what God revealed to Paul in Christ in that instant became the framework of Paul's thinking about Christ. Henceforth, Paul would speak about Jesus as "the Son of God" (Gal 1:16; Acts 9:20; cf. 1 Thess 1:10; 2 Cor 1:19; Rom 1:4); as the "highly exalted . . . Lord" (Acts 9:5; 22:10; 26:15; Phil 2:9, 11; 2 Cor 4:5); as "the image of God" (2 Cor 3:18; 4:4); as "glorious" (Acts 22:11; 9:3; 22:6; 2 Cor 4:4,

6); and as "the man of heaven" (1 Cor 15:49).

To say that the Damascus road event radically changed the direction of Paul's life is to tell only part of the story; his view of who Christ was entered into and became a permanent part of his thinking at that point. While for Paul the focus of interest was always the heavenly Lord, he knew certain things about the historical Lord. It is those historical details that concern us in this chapter.

We turn to the second word, *paradosis* ("tradition"). *Paradosis* means "a handing over," as of a prisoner from one jailer to another or of a piece of information from a teacher to a pupil. It was used in this latter sense of a lesson or teaching which a rabbi would impart to his disciple. Thus the rabbis handed over their teachings intact, generation by generation, to their pupils, who would in turn become rabbis. The usual English translation "traditions," a word that is often taken to mean "old things," fails to capture the dynamic "handing over" idea that is intrinsic to *paradosis*.

THE TRADITIONS: FROM WHOM DID PAUL RECEIVE THEM?

In the course of time Paul would, like a rabbi, hand over important pieces of information (*paradoseis*) about Jesus to the churches. First, however, he had to receive them from those who were Christian teachers before him. In writing to the Corinthians Paul mentions both the "receiving" and the "delivering" of the *paradosis* about the gospel:

I delivered to you . . . what I also received. (1 Cor 15:3)

Earlier in this letter he repeated what he "delivered" to the Corinthians about the Last Supper, having previously "received" it from the Lord.

I received from the Lord what I also delivered to you, that the Lord Jesus on the night when he was betrayed took bread. (1 Cor 11:23)

This passage is striking. It refers both to the heavenly Lord ("the Lord") from whom Paul received the *paradosis* and also the historical Lord ("the Lord Jesus"). The heavenly Lord is seen as the one from whom Paul received the *paradosis*, even though it originated in history with the historical Lord who "on the night he was betrayed took bread."

What Paul omits to tell us is through whom he received that *paradosis*. I assume it to be the same person(s) from whom Paul received the *paradosis* about the gospel, mentioned above. When did Paul receive these *paradoseis* and from whom?

Paul's first contact as a Christian with other Christians was in Damascus immediately following his momentous encounter with Christ on the way there (Acts 9 and 22). Ananias told Paul to "be baptized and wash away your sins, calling on his name" (Acts 22:16).[2]

Paul was thrust straight away into a new world in which he had to learn about baptism, forgiveness, the name of Jesus (his deity), faith and doubtless many other things as well. Most likely it was in Damascus that Paul received the *paradoseis* about the gospel and the Lord's Supper since it was from that time he began to preach Jesus as the Son of God and as the Christ (Acts 9:20-22).

From whom, then, did Paul receive further information about the historical Jesus? So far as we can see, Paul himself had neither seen nor heard Jesus of Nazareth. Nevertheless he was converted soon after the resurrection, most likely within a year.[3] Therefore, his contact with Christians in Damascus (Acts 9:19) was very close in time to Jesus of Nazareth. Paul was an early convert to Christianity.

Within three years of his conversion (Gal 1:18 = Acts 9:26), he came to Jerusalem where he "visited" Peter and "saw" James. This is not to suggest that the stories and sayings of Jesus had all been systematically collected by the time of Paul's first visit to Jerusalem.

His second visit was made fourteen years after his conversion (Gal 2:1 = Acts 21:17), that is, in c. 47. It is reasonable to assume that some of the sources referred to by Luke (1:2) and found within Luke's and Matthew's Gospels were finalized by that time. It may also be assumed that Paul came to be aware of these sources on this and subsequent visits to Jerusalem (c. 49—Acts 15:4; c. 52—18:22).

If one bridge from Paul to the historical Jesus was his contact with the Jerusalem church through visits in c. 36, 47, 49 and 52, another was through his association outside Jerusalem with Barnabas, whose membership in the Jerusalem church went back to the earliest times (Acts 4:36-37).

Barnabas was in daily contact with Paul for four or five years (Acts 11:25, 30; 12:25; 13:1—14:28; 15:2, 4, 12, 36-39). Barnabas, whose conversion was closer in time to Christ than Paul's and who had been for a decade and a half in the fellowship of the original companions of Jesus, must have talked often to Paul about the historical Lord.

In sum, Paul had many opportunities to receive the *paradoseis* of the Jerusalem church and to learn about the life and teachings of Jesus of Nazareth.

It has been shown that the close correlation between certain well-defined sections in Paul's writings, for example Romans 12—14, with the reports of the teaching of Jesus, from the common source which lies behind Luke 6:27-38 and Matthew 5:38-48, is evidence that Paul had access to such teachings and passed them on to the Gentile churches.[4] Paul's prayer to God as "Abba" (Rom 8:15; Gal 4:6) clearly derives from Jesus (see Mk 14:36), as does a probable reference to the Lord's Prayer in the expression "Forbearing one another and . . . forgiving each other" (Col 3:13). Some scholars believe that Paul refers to the rural imagery of Jesus, as well as to the parables.[5]

THE HISTORICAL JESUS: HIS BIRTH AND DEATH

Birth and death are fundamental to human experience. A modern biographer is interested in the details surrounding the birth and death of his chief character. While only two Evangelists describe the birth of Jesus, all four enter into great detail about his death. The apostle Paul, however, supplies no historical details about either the birth or the death of Jesus.

What Paul dwells on is the fact and the meaning of the birth and death of Jesus, which are all of a piece in this famous sentence:

> For you know the grace of our Lord Jesus Christ, that though he was rich, yet for your sake he became poor, so that by his poverty you might become rich. (2 Cor 8:9)

Here we see the fact of his incarnation and death ("he became poor") and its meaning ("the grace of our Lord Jesus Christ"), but no historical details are given.

In Paul's thought the coming of Jesus into the world was necessary so that he might die. Thus, "When the time had fully come, God sent forth his

Son, born of [a] woman, born under the law, to redeem" (Gal 4:4-5). Paul knew that Jesus was brought up as a strict Jew ("born under the law"). The absence of reference to Jesus' father may mean that Paul knew of the virgin birth of Christ.

The fact and meaning of the death of the historical Lord are set out powerfully in the statement:

> For our sake [God] made him to be sin who knew no sin, so that in him we might become the righteousness of God. (2 Cor 5:21)

Notice that although no historical details are supplied in these statements about Jesus' birth and death, they appear to be known by the writer.

Thus, "he became poor" (2 Cor 8:9) is entirely consistent with the details in the nativity stories of Matthew and Luke. The general comment "born of a woman" implies that the writer knew specifically which woman. In relation to the death of Jesus, the apostle often refers to crucifixion as the mode of execution (Gal 3:1), and many have seen in the words "[God] made [Jesus] to be sin" an allusion to Jesus' cry from the cross (Mk 15:34). The way Paul speaks of the fact and the meaning of the birth and death of Jesus implies some knowledge of historical details, which, however, he does not supply.

THE HISTORICAL JESUS: HIS LIFE

Paul gives only a few details from the life of Jesus:

1. He descended from Abraham (Gal 3:16).
2. He was a Son of David (Rom 1:3).
3. He was naturally born but [perhaps?] supernaturally conceived (Gal 4:4).
4. He was born and lived under the Jewish law (Gal 4:4).
5. He welcomed people (Rom 15:5, 7).
6. His lifestyle was one of humility and service (Phil 2:7-8).
7. He was abused and insulted during his life (Rom 15:3).
8. He had a brother named James (Gal 1:19) and other brothers (1 Cor 9:5).
9. His disciple Peter was married (1 Cor 9:5; cf. Mk 1:30).

10. He instituted a memorial meal on the night of his betrayal (1 Cor 11:23-25).
11. He was betrayed (1 Cor 11:23).
12. He gave testimony before Pontius Pilate (1 Tim 6:13).
13. He was killed by Jews of Judea (1 Thess 2:14-15).
14. He was buried, rose on the third day and was thereafter seen alive on a number of occasions by many witnesses (1 Cor 15:4-8).

Although the information is limited, it is noteworthy in two ways.

First, the details are conveyed incidentally and innocently. It seems that if another theological point were to be made, the author was capable of introducing further historical facts. The implication is that Paul the apostle knew more about the historical Jesus than he says; presumably he saw no need to give further information.

Second, the Gospel narratives confirm every detail Paul gives, without exception. His statements are free of exaggeration or distortion. This is all the more impressive because Paul's chief focus was not the historical, but the heavenly, Lord.

THE HISTORICAL JESUS: HIS TEACHINGS

The apostle Paul reproduces relatively few of the teachings of Jesus in full. On the other hand, there are numerous snippets of teachings that will appear in the final versions of the Gospels; Paul was quoting from collections of teachings then in circulation.

The Lord's Supper	1 Corinthians 11:23-25; cf. Mark 14:22-25
Divorce and remarriage	1 Corinthians 7:10-11; cf. Mark 10:1-12
The laborer deserves wages	1 Corinthians 9:14; cf. Matthew 10:10; Luke 10:7
Eat what is set before you	1 Corinthians 10:27; cf. Luke 10:7
Tribute to whom due	Romans 13:7; cf. Mark 12:13-17
Thief in the night	1 Thessalonians 5:2-5; cf. Luke 12:39, 40

In addition to these more direct sayings, Paul makes numerous indirect allusions to the teachings of Jesus. For example:

Practical ethics	Romans 12:9—13:10; cf. Matthew 5—7
The return of Jesus	1-2 Thessalonians; cf. Matthew 24

It is beyond the scope of this work to enter into details at this point. The interested reader is referred to F. F. Bruce, *Paul, Apostle of the Free Spirit*, pages 100-112. The comments made about the life of the historical Jesus are true here also. First, Paul is able to give information as the need arises. Apparently what is listed above does not exhaust Paul's knowledge of the teachings of Jesus. Second, what we read in Paul of the words of Jesus is confirmed in the Gospels. At points where we can check him, Paul proves trustworthy, as the reader will observe as he examines the comparative references.

THE HISTORICAL JESUS: HIS ATTRIBUTES

The apostle Paul was aware of the personal attributes of the historical Jesus. As need arose, he exhorted his readers to live and act according to the example of Jesus. Let us consider how Paul used the known character of Jesus in his ministry to four groups of readers.

The Roman Christians. The Roman Christians were divided into ethnic groups each of which was divided against the other groups. Paul therefore wrote, "Let each of us please his neighbor for his good. . . . For Christ did not please himself" (Rom 15:2-3). Paul's reference to the obedient behavior of Christ (he "did not please himself"), reminds us of the statement of Christ, "I seek not my own will but the will of him who sent me" (Jn 5:30).

Paul, therefore, told those racially segregated Romans, "Welcome one another, therefore, as Christ has welcomed you" (Rom 15:7). Christ often used words of welcome, particularly to people in need; for instance: "Come to me . . . and I will give you rest" (Mt 11:28).

The Philippians. A second group, the Philippians, were behaving proudly in their dealings with one another. Paul encouraged them to "have this mind among yourselves, which is yours in Christ Jesus. . . . He humbled himself" (Phil 2:5, 8).

Once more we see Paul putting to people the example of Jesus. In the famous invitation "come to me," quoted above, Jesus went on to say, "I am gentle and lowly in heart" (Mt 11:29). Paul's "he humbled himself" is from the same Greek word-group as Jesus' disclosure "I am lowly."

The Corinthians. A third group of readers, the Corinthians, spurned Paul's style of ministry as weak. In reply he states: "I, Paul, myself entreat you, by the meekness and gentleness of Christ" (2 Cor 10:1).

The word "meekness" is basically the same as "gentle," the other word in Matthew 11:29 quoted above. Thus Jesus' words about himself being "gentle" and "lowly," as quoted in Matthew 11:29, are twice drawn upon by Paul, yet in such an inconspicuous way that the point is easily missed.

In his first letter to the Corinthians, Paul urges the readers to "seek" the good of their neighbors, "that they may be saved." Again, Christ is given as the example: "Be imitators of me, as I am of Christ" (1 Cor 11:1). These words remind us of Jesus' important statement to the tax collector, Zacchaeus: "For the Son of man came to seek and to save the lost" (Lk 19:10). In using the words "seek" and "save," Paul has echoed the sense of purpose we find in these words of Jesus.

The Galatians. The apostle told a fourth group of readers, the Galatians, about the love of Christ, "the Son of God, who loved me and gave himself for me" (Gal 2:20; cf. 2 Cor 5:14).

It was the fourth Evangelist who drew particular attention to the love of Jesus in his death for sinners. On the evening before the crucifixion Jesus acted out the meaning of love by washing the feet of the disciples. John commented: "having loved his own who were in the world, he loved them to the end" (Jn 13:1). Had Paul discussed these matters with John at the missionary "summit" in Jerusalem c. 47 (cf. Gal 2:7-9)? While the apostle Paul apparently wrote before the Gospels were completed, it is quite possible that in his several visits to Jerusalem he became aware of sources that would in time become part of the finished Gospels. Paul displays comprehensive understanding of the character of the historical Jesus—his obedience, his gracious welcome, his meekness and humility, his love for sinners and his desire to save them. Everything Paul affirms about the attributes of Jesus can be confirmed from the Gospels.

In speaking of the character of the historical Jesus, however, the apostle is not referring to a figure of the remote past. The historical Lord through death and resurrection is now the heavenly Lord who has taken his spiritual and emotional personality intact with him to the right hand of the Father. Sometimes Christians find it difficult to imagine what their Lord is like and they do not know how to approach him. The one who is now our heavenly

Lord was once the historical Lord. He reacted to suffering with compassion and to injustice with anger. Jesus displayed a wide range of human emotions; and he was both meek and majestic. The point is, as he was, so he is; he is now what he was then. We relate to him now as if we were relating to him then. The heavenly Lord has the same personal attributes as the historical Lord.

Although primarily interested in Jesus as his contemporary, heavenly Lord, the apostle Paul was by no means unaware of the career of the historical Lord. Through the *paradoseis* or "traditions" about Jesus, received from those who had been eyewitnesses of the Lord, Paul supplies information about the birth, life, death, personal attributes and sayings of Christ. Paul's facts, while not extensive, when checked against the Gospels prove to be correct in every case. It is clear that Paul did not manufacture details about Jesus or exaggerate what details he had. Paul's use of historical evidence was, it appears, both careful and sober.

FURTHER READING

F. F. Bruce, *Paul, Apostle of the Heart Set Free* (Grand Rapids: Eerdmans, 1978).

W. D. Davies, *Paul and Rabbinic Judaism* (Philadelphia: Fortress, 1980).

Archibald M. Hunter, *Paul and His Predecessors* (London: SCM Press, 1961).

Seyoon Kim, *The Origin of Paul's Gospel* (Grand Rapids: Eerdmans, 1981).

The Acts of
the Apostles

Luke's second volume, the book of Acts, covers a period of about thirty years (c. 33 to c. 63), the first thirty years of the history of Christianity. But how accurate, how trustworthy, is the book of the Acts of the Apostles in its account of this critical era?

Before answering that question, it is important to establish the following point. Like the Gospels, Acts must be understood on its own terms. Herein lies the problem. From early times it has been common to require this book to be something it is not.

What Is the Book of Acts?
In the latter half of the second century a list of New Testament books was compiled in Rome, with comments on authorship and origin. The Muratorian Canon (named after its modern publisher, Ludovico Muratori) says: "The Acts . . . of all the Apostles are written in one book." Evidently the fifth book of the New Testament was already known by that name, or something like it, when the Muratorian Canon was written. But how correct was it to designate the book by that title, or even the shorter version by which we now refer to it?

Although the names of the apostles are given at the beginning, only one of the Twelve, Peter, is involved in the narrative, and he virtually fades out of the picture after chapter 12. For the remainder of Acts the spotlight falls on one man, Luke's chief character, the apostle Paul. The author, in fact, did not set out to write about the deeds of *all* the apostles. Therefore the title as it stands is not entirely appropriate.

It is also misleading to regard this book as the history of Christianity for those three decades. Since the author makes no such claim for Acts, it is unreasonable for others to try to force it into this mold. Even allowing for differences between modern and ancient histories, there are too many omissions of vital detail for Acts to be regarded as the first church history. The following examples will be sufficient to demonstrate this.

After Paul, newly converted, arrived in Damascus we read, "for several days he was with the disciples" (Acts 9:19). A modern historian would investigate who those disciples were and how they came to be at distant Damascus so early in the history of Christianity. A near contemporary like Josephus might offer some comment, but not Luke. Even more striking is Luke's failure to explain the origins of Christians in Phoenicia (Acts 15:3), Puteoli (Acts 28:14) or Rome (Acts 28:15). One sentence from Luke about the beginnings of Christianity in Rome would have saved hundreds of pages of speculation in the centuries that followed.

A second example is Paul's list of sufferings in 2 Corinthians:

Five times I have received at the hands of the Jews the forty lashes less one. Three times I have been beaten with rods; once I was stoned. Three times I have been shipwrecked. (2 Cor 11:24-25)

Apart from the flogging and imprisonment of Paul in Philippi (Acts 16:22-24), Luke gives no information about those experiences, and yet we do not doubt that they occurred. Such omissions raise serious questions as to whether Luke set out to write a comprehensive history of the first decades of Christianity.

If Acts is not a book about the deeds of the apostles or the history of the church c. A.D. 33-63, what is it?

AIM OF ACTS

I hesitate to add more words to the volumes of opinion about the aims of the author of Acts, especially in a modest book like this. However, in answering the question about Luke's purposes in writing we must look in a straightforward way at his finished product. What do we discover? As we read, we can discern two closely connected primary emphases.

First, we notice that the story told in Acts begins in Jerusalem and ends in Rome. To the Jew, Jerusalem was the center, while Rome was the "ends of the earth" (see Acts 1:8; cf. Psalm of Solomon 8:15). To the Gentile, as most likely Theophilus (Acts 1:1) was,[1] Rome was the hub of the inhabited world. The author recounts how the gospel broke out of Jerusalem into Judea and from Judea to Samaria and from Samaria to the Gentiles and ultimately to Rome. In Acts he tells the story, through a series of smaller stories, of the triumphant procession of the preaching of the kingdom from Jerusalem to Rome.

Second, it becomes clear that the author wants us to understand that the bearer of God's word to the Gentiles and to the Gentile world capital was Paul. Certainly Peter is prominent in the early stories, but after the Jerusalem Council (Acts 15:7-11) he does not reappear. Luke shows us first how Peter brought the gospel to the Gentiles (Acts 9:32—10:47). Then he shows us how Paul brought the gospel to the Gentiles (beginning Acts 13:1 but see particularly 13:46-47). If Peter, who brought the gospel to the Gentiles, was an apostle, then Paul also was an apostle (Acts 14:4, 14). There is evidence that sections of the Jewish Christian community were bent on telling the Gentiles that Paul was not a genuine apostle (see 1 Cor 9:2; 2 Cor 12:12). That Luke describes Christ's call of Paul not once, not twice, but three times (Acts 9:1-9; 22:3-21; 26:2-23), shows that the author desired to establish Paul's credentials as the apostle to the Gentiles.

While Luke had lesser aims in writing, these two are, I believe, his main ones. But how does he achieve his objectives?

Consider the first chapter. The author could have written:

> Due to the treachery and the death of Judas there was a vacancy in the apostolic company. The Christians met and appointed Matthias to fill the vacancy.[2]

But no. Luke conveys this information by means of a story told in such a way that we can see it in our minds. As we read on we find that Acts is a series of dramatic stories. This is not simply to make his narrative more interesting. There is the deeper intention to "edify" the readers.[3] As in the case of the Gospels, the writer is addressing the will and the emotions, not merely the intellect.

The essential character of Acts is expressed in the very first sentence:

> In the first book, O Theophilus, I have dealt with all that Jesus began to do and teach, until the day when he was taken up.

We are meant to understand this to be a second book in which the author deals with all that Jesus will *continue* to do and teach after the day he was taken up. If the opening words anticipate the deeds and teachings of the ascended Jesus, the book as it unfolds by means of connected stories tells how Paul, the "chosen instrument" of the glorified Lord (Acts 9:15), would bring the word of God to the Gentiles and to Rome (Acts 26:16-18).

HOW TRUSTWORTHY?

There are four reasons, in particular, which encourage us to have a high regard for the historical trustworthiness of the Acts of the Apostles.

Luke's proven use of sources. Paul is the chief character of Acts, with Peter playing an important, but lesser, role. In describing what happened, the author will usually write "Peter . . . he" or "Paul . . . he." Where Peter or Paul are with companions the plural pronoun "they" is used.

There are three passages, however, when the pronoun "we" is used. This means that the author of Luke-Acts has become part of his narrative, along with Paul and his companions. The three "we" passages are

Acts 16:10-16	Journey from Troas to Philippi in c. 50
Acts 20:5—21:17	Journey from Philippi to Jerusalem in c. 57
Acts 27: 1—28:14	Journey from Caesarea to Rome in c. 60

These three passages supply a wealth of information about places, people and time. They are the most detailed passages of the whole of Acts, as one would expect, because the author was an eyewitness of what he describes. Consider, for example, the concentration of historical detail in Luke's account of Paul's journey from Caesarea to Rome in Acts 27:1 to 28:14, the final "we" passage.

Where did the author find the information for the other parts of Acts? Since Luke was a traveling companion of Paul in the "we" passages, we suppose that Paul himself was Luke's source for those other passages that focus on Paul. A substantial part of Acts is taken up with the deeds of Paul—as a persecutor (7:58—8:3), as an early convert in Damascus (9:1-30), as a leader in the church in Antioch (11:25-30) and as a traveling missionary (12:25—28:31).

The remainder of the Acts of the Apostles is devoted to the early Christian community in Jerusalem and the spread of the gospel to other parts of Palestine.

What were Luke's sources of information for these earliest parts of his narrative? Unfortunately he does not identify the people or documents on whom he depended. It is clear, however, that Luke met people who could have supplied the raw material for his book. In the second of the "we" passages, describing the journey from Philippi to Jerusalem, the author met three men who were present in the early days of Christianity in Palestine. At Caesarea Luke met the prophet Agabus (21:10) who was active in the Jerusalem church in the middle forties. Also at Caesarea, Paul and Luke stayed with Philip the evangelist (21:8), who was a Hellenist Christian from the early thirties and who himself subsequently evangelized the Samaritans and the coastal region from Azotus to Caesarea. On their arrival in Jerusalem Paul and Luke stayed with Mnason, a Cypriot, who had been a disciple from the earliest times (21:16). Luke's contact with Agabus, Philip and Mnason could well have provided considerable information for the narrative that Luke would one day write. Doubtless there were many opportunities for Luke to seek information from other people in Jerusalem and Caesarea during Paul's two-year imprisonment in Caesarea. If Peter were in Rome when Luke and Paul arrived in the early sixties, Luke would have had further opportunities to gather information for the story of those early years in Jerusalem.

Not to be overlooked as a source of Luke's information about the early years in Jerusalem is Paul himself. Paul makes it quite clear that he met James, Peter, John and Barnabas, who would have passed on considerable information to Paul.

Fortunately there are two ways we can check Luke's accuracy in using sources. As we shall see, one is the care with which he uses information supplied by the apostle Paul. The other, as we have already seen, is the sober way he handles the text of Mark's Gospel, much of which he incorporates within his own. Although we have no means of crosschecking the ways in which we suppose Luke used information from Agabus, Philip and Mnason, his credibility is so strong at the points where he can be checked that we may have confidence in his integrity at those points where we have no way to check him.

Information about Paul in Acts. There is a certain amount of historical information about Paul to be found in the Acts of the Apostles, most of it in speeches attributed to Paul. Where could Luke have obtained this information except from Paul? The possibility that Luke had access to Paul's letters and gleaned his data from them is fairly unlikely. Paul's letters were not yet gathered into one collection, and in any case, Luke's style and vocabulary show little evidence of being influenced by Paul's letters.

Let us consider the two classes of information about Paul in the Acts of the Apostles that can be checked in his letters.

First, there is the cluster of information relating to Paul's conversion and his early life as a Christian. The chief source from Paul is in Galatians, with some amplification in 2 Corinthians and Philippians. The corresponding passages in Acts are the narrative of his conversion in chapter 9 and the two autobiographical speeches in chapters 22 and 26 (see pp. 152-53).

Paul's confirmation of the Acts information relating to the broad outline of his conversion and early career is striking, the more so since the author of Acts apparently did not have access to Paul's letters. However, it would not be true to suggest that there were no problems in the dovetailing of Acts and Paul. Acts, for example, omits any reference to Paul's sojourn in Arabia (see Gal 1:17). Moreover, Acts attributes the danger in Damascus to the Jews (Acts 9:23) whereas in Paul it is the governor of the Arabian king Aretas from whom Paul escapes (2 Cor 11:32-33). According to Acts, Paul went in and out among the apostles in Jerusalem (Acts 9:28) whereas in Galatians, the only apostles with whom Paul conferred were Cephas and James (Gal 1:18-19). In Acts Paul states that he evangelized throughout all the country of Judea (Acts 26:19-20), while in Galatians 1:22 he writes that he was not known by sight to the churches of Judea.

It is possible that each and every one of these discrepancies could be harmonized if we possessed more complete documentation. It must always be remembered that Acts is no more a straight biography of Paul than his own letters are autobiographical. In both Acts and Paul's letters historical details, while important, are secondary and incidental. On the face of it, then, the broad sequence of these early events, as found in Acts, is confirmed by Paul's letters, while at the same time there are a number of awkward but minor discrepancies.

The second class of information found in Acts, which also appears in Paul's letters, concerns four miscellaneous incidents or movements during the subsequent stages of his missionary career. These can be stated briefly.

One relates to what was apparently Paul's second visit as a Christian to Jerusalem, fourteen years after his conversion. While Acts gives the reason for the visit as famine relief (Acts 11:27-30), Paul states that it was to hold a private meeting with James, Peter and John (Gal 2:1-10). There is no good reason to doubt that both sources are describing the same visit.

Another relates to the incident in Antioch after Paul's return from his missionary tour of Galatia. Both Acts (15:2) and Galatians (2:12-13) refer to a serious dispute between Paul and certain visitors from Jerusalem. Although the two sources give, on the face of it, different grounds for the dispute, there can be little doubt that Galatians 2:11-14 corroborates Acts 15:1-2.

Describing the second missionary tour, Acts narrates Paul's visit to Philippi, Thessalonica, Athens and Corinth along with the movements of his colleagues Timothy and Silas (Acts 16:12; 17:1, 15; 18:1, 5). Details are corroborated in Paul's first letter to the Thessalonians (2:1-2; 3:1-6; cf. 2 Cor 1:19).

There was also the journey from Ephesus to Macedonia at the end of the third missionary journey (Acts 20:1), which is confirmed by Paul in the second Corinthian letter (2 Cor 2:12-13).

We may say, with both classes of data in mind, that although neither author was primarily attempting to write a history, and although there are some loose ends in those places where the data overlaps, the details in Paul's letters amply corroborate the broad historicity of the Acts of the Apostles.

We return to our question: Where could Luke have obtained his information about Paul, except from Paul? We have excluded the letters of Paul as the source of data. Paul himself was Luke's source for both kinds of information. As Paul's traveling companion in c. 50 and c. 57, Luke had ample opportunity to find out about Paul's earlier journeys. With regard to the information about Paul's career as a Pharisee and persecutor, followed by his conversion and early ministry, we should note that Luke may well have been present when Paul delivered the speeches in Acts 22 and 26 setting forth the information. Paul's letters, and the historical details they contain, remain an objective measure of the care with which Luke incorporated into Acts the verbal details almost certainly supplied by Paul.

	PAUL'S LETTERS	ACTS NARRATIVE
His "former life in Judaism" (Gal 1:13)	Are they Israelites? So am I. (2 Cor 11:22) As to the law a Pharisee. (Phil 3:5)	I am a Jew. (22:3) I have lived as a Pharisee. (26:5)
Zealous persecutor	As to zeal a persecutor of the church. (Phil 3:6)	Being zealous for God . . . I persecuted this Way to the death. (22:3-4)
God's call	[God] called me, . . . was pleased to reveal his Son to me. (Gal 1:15-16)	At Damascus . . . he proclaimed Jesus, saying, "He is the Son of God." (9:19-20)
Sent to the Gentiles	[God] . . . called me . . . that I might preach [his Son] among the Gentiles. (Gal 1:15-16)	"I am Jesus. . . . I have appeared . . . to appoint you to . . . witness to the things in which you have seen me . . . the Gentiles—to whom I send you." (26:15-17)

	PAUL'S LETTERS	ACTS NARRATIVE
Early ministry in Damascus	At Damascus . . . I was let down in a basket. (2 Cor 11:32-33; cf. Gal 1:17)	At Damascus . . . his disciples . . . let [Paul] down over the wall . . . in a basket. (9:19, 25)
First visit to Jerusalem	Then after three years I went up to Jerusalem. (Gal 1:18)	When he had come to Jerusalem . . . (9:26)
Danger in Judea	[The Jews] drove us out [of Judea]. (1 Thess 2:14-15)	The Hellenists . . . were seeking to kill him. (9:29)
Withdrawal to Syria-Cilicia	Then I went into the regions of Syria and Cilicia. (Gal 1:21)	They brought him to Caesarea, and sent him off to Tarsus. (9:30)

External events. The most remarkable external corroboration of the historicity of Acts relates to Paul's ministry in Corinth. When he arrived there he met Aquila and Priscilla who were

> lately come from Italy . . . because Claudius had commanded all the Jews to leave Rome. (Acts 18:2)

Suetonius, the Roman historian, refers to this event that occurred in Rome c. 49:

> Since the Jews constantly made disturbances at the instigation of Chrestus [sic] he [Claudius] expelled them from Rome. (*Life of Claudius* 25.4)

Luke and Suetonius unconsciously corroborate each other's accounts.

Aquila and Priscilla must have arrived in Corinth in A.D. 49 or later. Since Paul came there after them, we may fix A.D. 49 as the earliest possible time for his arrival in Corinth. As it happens, we are also able to establish the latest possible date for Paul's arrival in Corinth. Earlier this century an inscription was discovered at Delphi in Greece that noted the appointment of Gallio as proconsul of Achaia (the province of which Corinth was the capital) in July 51.[4] Paul, therefore, must have come to Corinth somewhere between 49 and 51, in all probability late in the year 50. Thus the interlocking pieces of evidence from Suetonius and Delphi exactly confirm Luke's account of Paul's period in Corinth.

The Acts accounts describe Paul standing before the tribunal or *bema* (Acts 18:12), on which Gallio the governor sat conducting the court hearing. Archaeologists have discovered in the forum of Corinth a speaker's platform that elsewhere is referred to as the *rosta*, a Latin word corresponding to the Greek *bema*. It was, doubtless, before this platform that the apostle Paul stood before Gallio in A.D. 51.

While this is the most extensive pattern of information external to Acts, it is by no means alone. The narrative refers to the high priests Annas (4:6) and Ananias (23:2); Herod Agrippa I (12:1-3, 20, 23); Herod Agrippa II (25:13—26:32); Sergius Paulus, proconsul of Cyprus (13:7); the Egyptian prophet (21:38); and the procurators Felix (23:23—24:27) and Festus (24:27). Each of these persons is referred to in sources outside the New Testament.

Since Luke proves to be so accurate with these well-known persons, we may reasonably express confidence in his references to lesser persons about whom the major historical sources make no mention—Simon the magician (8:9), the centurion Cornelius (10:1—11:18), Antipas's courtier Manaen (13:1), Elymas the magician (13:8), Dionysius the Areopagite (17:34), Demetrius the silversmith (19:24), the tribune Claudius Lysias (23:26), the advocate Tertullus (24:1, 2), the centurion Julius (27:1) and Publius the chief man of Malta (28:7). The list of public figures, some major and some minor, is impressive.

There can be no doubt that while Acts does not purport to be the history of primitive Christianity, it is nevertheless historical in character.

It would not be true, however, to say there are no problems in Luke's double-volumed work.[5] Two, in particular, deserve mention.

In Gamaliel's speech to the Sanhedrin he states, "Before these days Theu-

das arose. . . . After him Judas the Galilean arose" (Acts 5:36-37). "Judas the
Galilean" is straightforward. He led an uprising at the changeover of government in Judea from the Herods to the Romans that occurred in A.D. 6. The
only "Theudas" known to historical records was a prophet who arose c. A.D.
45, that is, not "before" but "after" Judas. Many accuse Luke of error at this
point. Theudas, however, was not an uncommon name, and the period before A.D. 6 was very turbulent, especially after the death of Herod in 4 B.C.
Indeed, had he placed Theudas after Judas, Luke would be really open to
criticism, since Gamaliel's speech occurred about ten years before the Theudas known to historians. As it stands, given Luke's care in other areas where
he can be checked and the lack of information about Theudas, it is better to
give Luke the benefit of the doubt.

The other and more serious matter is the author's statement about the
birth of Jesus:

> In those days a decree went out from Caesar Augustus that all the
> world should be enrolled. This was the first enrollment, when Quirin-
> ius was governor of Syria. (Lk 2:1-2; cf. Acts 5:37)

The problem is that, according to Josephus (*Antiquities* 18:1-2), Quirinius
conducted an enrollment in Judea at the time of the changeover from
Herodian to Roman rule in A.D. 6. But Matthew (2:1) as well as Luke himself
(1:5-28) place the birth of Jesus in the days of Herod the Great, who died in
4 B.C. On the face of it, Luke 2:1-2 is astray by approximately ten years.
While the words "first enrollment" may be taken to refer to an enrollment
prior to the more famous occurrence of A.D. 6, complete and continuous
records of governors in Syria leave no room for Quirinius to have been governor at an earlier date. Many scholars have seized on this verse as evidence
of Luke's inaccuracy in historical matters. This is hardly fair. In the Greek
original so few words are used that it can be translated in several ways. The
version, "This was an enrollment *before* Quirinius was governor of Syria" is
less attractive grammatically, but it is quite consistent historically with Luke's
own fixing of the birth of Jesus in the days of Herod. There is good reason
to leave this question open pending the availability of more evidence before
sweepingly rejecting Luke's competence as a historian.

The problems in Luke must be kept in proper perspective. The areas of serious difficulty are limited to two or three which are, in each case, highly complex. On the other hand, on the numerous occasions where Luke has committed himself to specific details he can be shown to be accurate. The great archaeologist Sir William Ramsay once commented: "Luke's history is unsurpassed in respect of its trustworthiness."[6]

The trivia of Acts. Much of Paul's work, as recorded in Acts, occurred in the Roman provinces of Cyprus, Galatia, Asia, Macedonia and Achaia. After they conquered a region, the Romans wisely allowed local methods of government to continue for a period. Writing of the era in which Acts describes Paul's labors, E. A. Judge comments:

> The standardization of government had by no means worked itself out, nor was Roman control yet evenly imposed in every quarter. The Acts of the Apostles is a kaleidoscope of local diversity.[7]

The eminent Roman historian A. N. Sherwin-White has examined incidental references in the Acts to trials, punishment, city government and citizenship. In case after case he finds that the "narrative agrees with the evidence of the earlier period." In summary, Sherwin-White states about the Acts: "Any attempt to reject its basic historicity even in matters of detail must now appear absurd."[8]

Acts indeed captures the sense of local diversity referred to above, as three examples will demonstrate.

In Thessalonica the decisions about Paul were made by "the Politarchs" (Acts 17:6, 8), a word that appears rarely in ancient books. The inscription over the archway of the Vandar Gate at Thessalonica, now in the British Museum, reads "In the time of the Politarchs," thus demonstrating Luke's accurate attention to detail. Similarly, in the account of the riot in Ephesus, capital of Asia, Luke refers to "the Asiarchs" who begged Paul not to enter the theater (Acts 19:31). Strabo, who wrote about the geography of the times, referred to "the Asiarchs . . . the first men of their province" (14.1.42). Finally, on the island of Malta Luke's reference to "the chief man of the island, named Publius" (Acts 28:7) is confirmed by an inscription which reads "Pudens, equite of the Romans, chief man of Malta" (*Inscriptiones Graecae*

14.601). Space prevents the citation of more evidence, but enough has been presented to make the point that Luke carefully preserves the detailed accuracy of local customs of government.

The answer to the question "How trustworthy is the Acts of the Apostles?" is "Very trustworthy"—provided we don't try to force the book into molds of our own making rather than Luke's. The book does not set out to narrate all that the apostles did nor is it a comprehensive account of earliest church history. What Luke sets out to show us, in an edifying and not merely informative way, is how the word of God came from the Jewish capital Jerusalem to the Gentile capital Rome, thus vindicating its bearer Paul as the apostle to the Gentiles.

Let us read what two scholars have written. They approach their study of Acts from different directions. Colin J. Hemer, in a painstaking study of what he calls "the trivia of Acts," comments:

> I have an interest here in the unimportant, in the nuances, which might betray a redactor's faulty knowledge of the context of a precise but unimportant statement. I submit that it is exceedingly hard to reproduce second hand, in one's own style, intricate reports of fact. Yet we can check the trivia of Acts against the inscriptions: "town clerk" at Ephesus, "politarchs" at Thessalonica, "first man" of Malta. . . . Less obvious but more pervasive are the marginal things, the incidence of personal names, the illustrations of customs in verbal uses. . . . And there is the factor of the subtle interlocking of pieces . . . the dates of the Gallio inscription . . . the expulsion of the Jews from Italy. . . . There are in fact incidentals . . . which contribute unemphatically to the building of a picture which correlates with external literature and with archaeology.[9]

Martin Hengel, on the other hand, has compared Acts with other "histories" written at that time. He notices that Luke, like other historians of antiquity, sometimes abbreviates, omits, elaborates or repeats when he writes. Hengel notes:

> All this can be found in the secular histories of Greek and Roman antiquity. On the other hand, one can hardly accuse him of simply hav-

ing invented events, created scenes out of nothing and depicted them on a broad canvas, deliberately falsifying his traditions in an unrestrained way for the sake of cheap effect. He is quite certainly not simply concerned with pious edification at the expense of truth. He is not just an "edifying writer," but a historian and theologian who needs to be taken seriously. His account always remains within the limits of what was considered reliable by the standards of antiquity.[10]

Is Acts historically trustworthy? Its attention to detail, as well as its observable style relative to that of other ancient histories, suggests that the answer is in the affirmative.

FURTHER READING

Martin Hengel, *Acts and the History of Earliest Christianity* (Philadelphia: Fortress, 1980).

I. Howard Marshall, *Luke: Historian and Theologian* (Grand Rapids: Zondervan, 1970).

William M. Ramsay, *St. Paul the Traveler and Roman Citizen* (Grand Rapids: Kregel, 2001).

A. N. Sherwin-White, *Roman Society and Roman Law in the New Testament* (Grand Rapids: Baker, 1978).

15

ARCHAEOLOGY AND THE NEW TESTAMENT

"Hard Copy" from Antiquity

For many years the lands of the Bible have been searched for inscriptions and other "hard copy" that would prove or disprove the accuracy of the New Testament narratives.

JESUS IN THE GOSPELS

Has anything been discovered that casts light on Jesus or the early disciples? The only such "light" was the "James" ossuary (coffin for bones) made public in 2002 bearing the Aramaic words, "James, son of Joseph, brother of Jesus." The words "brother of Jesus," while scientifically dated to that time, were not inscribed in the same hand as the other words, raising doubts as to their genuineness. Deception has been proposed, but it is difficult to explain why a forger at that time would add the words "brother of Jesus." Furthermore, a different writing style is not a fatal difficulty. Different handwriting appears on another ossuary from the same period, the Yehohanan ossuary mentioned shortly. Nonetheless, there is sufficient doubt about the James ossuary to suspend judgment on the authenticity of the reference to Jesus. This is the only (possible) direct light from archaeology on a central New Testament figure.

In 1961 a mosaic dated from the third century in which Nazareth appears was unearthed in Caesarea Maritima. Nazareth, home town of Jesus, is not mentioned in the Old Testament, nor in Josephus's works. Questions as to its genuineness were resolved by this discovery.

There is no shortage of light cast upon secondary figures who play a part in the Gospel narratives. There are coins bearing the names of the Herod family, for example, Herod the king (who killed the boys at the time of Jesus' birth), his son Herod the tetrarch of Galilee (who killed John the Baptist and whom Jesus called "that fox"), Herod's grandson Herod Agrippa I (who killed James Zebedee) and Herod's great-grandson Herod Agrippa II (before whom Paul gave testimony). These Herods are also well attested in the Jewish historian Josephus and to a lesser extent in the Roman historian Tacitus.

The Herods were great builders, notably Herod the king—also known as Herod "the Great"—who died when Jesus was just a few years old. Herod built great fortresses like Masada and the impressive seaport at Caesarea Maritima. He is most famous for building the vast temple in Jerusalem, destroyed by the Romans in the last months of the year 70. The stone platform covering many acres on which the temple stood, however, is still there, as are the massive walls supporting it, most famously the "western wall" revered by Jewish people.

Caiaphas the high priest and Pilate the governor, key participants in the trials and crucifixion of Jesus, have left behind evidence that has been unearthed in recent times. In 1990 an ossuary was discovered inscribed with the words in Aramaic, "Joseph son of Caiaphas." Caiaphas is also mentioned by Josephus. Earlier, in 1961, an inscription was found in Caesarea bearing the words in Latin, "Pontius Pilate, Prefect of Judaea." Pilate, though a relatively minor governor, is referred to at some length by Josephus and Philo and mentioned by Tacitus.

Archaeological evidence for those prominent people impressively locates the Gospels' account of Jesus in a genuine and imaginable historical context.

Another interesting discovery was made in 1941 in the Kidron valley in Jerusalem. It is an ossuary inscribed in Greek, "Alexander the Cyrene, son of Simon." This is most likely one and the same as the son of the bystander compelled to carry Jesus' cross, "Simon of Cyrene, . . . the father of Alexander and Rufus" (Mk 15:21).

The discovery of inscriptions is important; words carry clear meaning that mute artifacts do not. In 1956 an ossuary was found bearing words in Aramaic, "Everything that a man will find to his profit in this ossuary is an offering (*qorban*) to the Lord." This confirms the word "Corban" embedded in the Greek text of Mark 7:11 and Jesus' criticism of the "Corban" practice (see Mk 7:9-13).

Less spectacular, but still important, are items lacking identifying words. A fishing boat from Jesus' times has been located in Lake Galilee. Numerous anchors, hooks and sinkers have been found confirming the Gospels' portrayal of fishing and fishermen there. Housing has been excavated in Capernaum that appears to have been in use in Jesus' day. Various synagogues have been located in Galilee, for example, in Capernaum and Chorazin (built some years after Jesus).

In 1968 near Jerusalem an ossuary was discovered bearing the bones of a man named Yehohanan who had been killed in the twenties of the first century. Of great interest is that Yehohanan met his death by crucifixion, just a few years before Jesus was crucified. These are the only known remains of a man crucified in Roman Palestine. Yehohanan had been impaled by iron spikes through his hands to a crossbeam and through his ankles to the vertical stake. This grim discovery gives us an idea of the way the Roman death squad crucified Jesus.

In 1878 a marble slab came to light on which was inscribed in Greek a "decree of Caesar" forbidding the removal of human remains from tombs and graves, and warning of capital punishment for offenders. This is known as the "Nazareth Decree," though its place of discovery is unknown and the Roman emperor is not identified in the text. Granted that the "decree" is authentic, as it most likely is, how is it significant? If the "decree" predated the first Easter it would by itself make unlikely the claim that the disciples stole the body of Jesus (Mt 27:62-66; 28:11-15). To have done so would have meant death.

Discoveries of artifacts with words, especially words identifying known persons, are exciting and are reported in the media. Other discoveries are also important since they illuminate the life and times of Jesus and combine to establish a setting for his ministry as narrated in the Gospels.

THE EARLY CHURCH IN THE BOOK OF ACTS

An explicit artifact relating to early Christianity is an inscription bearing the name "Paullus Sergius," discovered in the eighties in Pisidian Antioch (Yalvac in modern Turkey). The highlight of Paul's mission to Cyprus in c. A.D. 47 was the conversion of the Roman governor, Sergius Paulus (Acts 13:4-12). From that time the book of Acts refers to Saul as "Paul." Possibly as a Roman citizen he had been given the Roman name "Paul" as his cognomen (nickname). However, this appears too much a coincidence. It is more likely that Saul adopted the name Paul to mark the conversion of this eminent Roman named Paul. Perhaps the governor himself gave Paul his name to establish some kind of patronage of the missionary.

Whatever the case, Paul and Barnabas traveled directly from Cyprus to Antioch in the region of Pisidia, near the southern border of Galatia. This was a major crossroads city and a Roman colony. It was also the district of the powerful Roman Paulli family to which the governor Cyprus belonged. This is now evident (since the 1980s) from not one but several inscriptions bearing the family name Paullus Sergius unearthed in Pisidian Antioch. It is possible that Paul came with letters of introduction to facilitate his ministry in that region. The Paullus Sergius inscription confirms the accuracy of the Acts narrative and may explain why Paul went past other possible centers for mission to the rather remote city, Colonia Antiocheia.

In Delphi in 1915 an inscription was found in which the emperor Claudius refers to "Gallio, my friend and Proconsul." This confirms the words of Acts 18:12-17 "when Gallio was proconsul of Achaia." The time note "when" is important since the Delphi inscription pinpoints Gallio's arrival to the year A.D. 51. Proconsuls were appointed by the Roman Senate and served for only a year, beginning July 1. The convergence of information from the Delphi inscription and Acts 18:12 establishes that Paul would have arrived in Corinth sometime in A.D. 50. This is an important benchmark for establishing New Testament chronology.

In Corinth there is another inscription bearing a name we meet in the New Testament, though this is less certain. A marble pavement near the theater in Corinth bears the name, "Erastus, commissioner for public works." In his letter to the Romans written from Corinth Paul sends greetings from "Erastus, the city treasurer" (16:23). Since the inscription is dated to the general period when Paul wrote Romans the identification is possible, despite the differing offices the men held. It was not unknown for men to hold several offices at different times. It is by no means unlikely that the Erastus in the inscription is the same one who appears in Paul's letter.

Other artifacts are less dramatic but contribute to the backdrop against which the story of early Christianity unfolds.

In 1913 an inscription was unearthed in the city of David to the south of the Old City in Jerusalem. Written in Greek the text commemorates the foundation of a synagogue and guesthouse for foreign Jews visiting Jerusalem for the major feasts. It states that the function of the synagogue was for "the reading of the Law and the teaching of the commandments." This inscription illuminates the text of the early chapters of Acts describing the Jews from the Diaspora visiting Jerusalem for Pentecost (Acts 2:5, 8-11). It also tends to confirm the presence in Jerusalem of Greek-speaking Jews, known as "Hellenists" (Acts 6:1, 5; 9:29).

Archaeological discoveries have tended to confirm the accuracy of the book of Acts and the author's "eye for detail." When the Romans conquered the old Hellenistic kingdoms in Greece and Asia Minor they tended to allow many existing administrative practices to continue. In the coming centuries these were standardized, but not in the first century.

Acts is sensitive to this diversity of local practice. This is evident in references to "Politarchs" in Thessalonica (Acts 17:8), to "Asiarchs" in Ephesus (Acts 19:31) and to the "First Man" in Malta (Acts 28:7). Inscriptions bearing these specific but varying titles have been discovered in Thessalonica, Ephesus and Malta, but not in other places.

In 1935 a limestone block was found in Jerusalem bearing this warning:

Let no Gentile enter
within the partition and barrier
surrounding the temple;
whosoever is caught shall be responsible
for his subsequent death.

Both Josephus and Philo mention this prohibition. More to the point is the complaint against Paul that "he . . . brought Greeks into the temple, and he has defiled this holy place" (Acts 21:28).

THE CONTRIBUTION OF ARCHAEOLOGY

From this brief and incomplete survey it is clear that archaeology neither proves nor disproves the New Testament. It does, however, endorse the narratives at many points, especially in the case of inscriptions, which by their nature are specific. Here we meet characters secondary to the main story—the Herods, the high priest and several Roman governors. Moreover, through archaeology we are able to fill in background details that enhance the narratives in both the Gospels and in the book of Acts. Archaeological findings have confirmed that the texts of the New Testament are from first to last historical and geographical in character.

FURTHER READING

F. F. Bruce, *Jesus and Christian Origins Outside the New Testament* (Grand Rapids: Eerdmans, 1974), pp. 187-202.

Craig A. Evans, "Jesus and the Ossuaries," *Bulletin for Biblical Research* 13, no. 1 (2003): 21-46.

Jack Finegan, *The Archeology of the New Testament: The Life of Jesus and the Beginning of the Early Church* (Princeton: Princeton University Press, 1969).

———, *The Archeology of the New Testament: The Mediterranean World of the Early Christian Apostles* (Boulder, Colo.: Westview Press, 1981).

Colin J. Hemer, *The Letters to the Seven Churches of Asia in their Local Setting* (Sheffield: JSOT, 1986).

———, "Luke the Historian," *Bulletin of the John Rylands Library* 60 (1977-1978): 28-51.

John McRay, *Archaeology and the New Testament* (Grand Rapids: Baker, 1991).

Steven Feldman and Nancy Roth, "The Short List: The New Testament Figures Known to History," *Biblical Archaeology Review* 28, no. 6 (2002): 34-37.

John J. Rousseau and Rami Arav, *Jesus and His World* (Minneapolis: Fortress, 1995).

George Adam Smith, *The Historical Geography of the Holy Land* (New York: Harper & Row, 1966).

16

IS THE NEW TESTAMENT HISTORICALLY RELIABLE?

L et us draw together the threads of the argument.

The aim of this book has been to examine the historical reliability of the New Testament. Most people want to know whether or not the New Testament is historically true before they can begin to think about believing its theological message. If they doubt the historical truth of the New Testament, that is the end of the matter.

We have not asked the reader to accept that New Testament documents are special in any religious way. The question of historical reliability can be discussed apart from the question of "inspiration," and that is what we have done.

Many readers will have been surprised to learn how much the Gospels, Acts and the autobiographical parts of Paul's letters have in common with ancient history writers like Thucydides or Josephus. Few, if any, of the history writers of antiquity wrote "pure" history to provide the reader with "mere" facts. Facts were presented, certainly, but to make a point. Thucydides, for example, wrote to provide "an exact knowledge of the past" which, he continued, would act "as an aid to the interpretation of the future" (*Peloponnesian War* 1.23). Thucydides provided a factual account but he had an underlying motive for writing.

The historian Josephus (c. A.D. 37-96), like most of the New Testament writers, was a Jew, and moreover, one whose life span overlapped Paul's. In the opening lines of the *Jewish War* Josephus stated his commitment to factual narration: "I . . . propose to provide the subjects of the Roman Empire with a narrative of the facts" (1:3). His deeper intentions, however, may be discerned in the following words:

> In my reflections on the events I cannot conceal my private senti-
> ments. . . . [M]y country . . . owed its ruin to civil strife. . . . [I]t was
> the Jewish tyrants who drew down upon the holy temple the unwill-
> ing hands of the Romans. (1:10)

What makes Josephus so interesting is his undoubted ability to provide detailed and factual information while at the same time presenting the readers with a sustained "case" against the revolutionaries among his fellow countrymen. Josephus's historical works greatly add to our knowledge of the Jewish people in the century in which Jesus lived and the early church was born.

This concern for facts, while at the same time making a point, may be discerned also in the Gospel writers, explicitly so in the cases of John and Luke. John, for example, stated with reference to the crucifixion, but in a manner that is true of this entire Gospel:

> He who saw it has borne witness—his testimony is true, and he knows
> that he tells the truth—that you also may believe. (Jn 19:35; cf. 21:24;
> 20:31)

John witnessed to "the truth" so that the reader (20:31) may "believe." For his part, Luke stated:

> It seemed good to me also, having followed all things closely [accu-
> rately?] for some time past, to write an orderly account for you . . . that
> you may know the truth concerning the things of which you have
> been informed. (Lk 1:3-4)

Luke researched the sources and wrote an orderly, chronologically accurate narrative, so that the reader might know that what Luke learned about Jesus, perhaps by word of mouth, is historically true. It will be remembered that Luke's words form an introduction to both his Gospel and the Acts of the Apostles.

The writers of the Gospels and Acts were people of their own times, as we are of ours. While the Gospels and Acts have many distinctive and innovative features, they are, in broad terms, recognizable as examples of the history writing of their period. It is both unhelpful and untrue to regard them merely as religious or theological works. They are also unmistakably historical in character. As historical sources for the period, the Gospels are as valuable to the general historian as Josephus, except that unlike Josephus they are focused on one person and a brief period. The eminent Roman historian A. N. Sherwin-White, for example, writes of our dependence on the parables of Jesus for an understanding of life in Galilee at that time:

> The pattern of life, both social and economic, civil and religious, is precisely what is to be expected in the isolated district of Galilee. . . . [T]he absence of Graeco-Roman colouring is a convincing feature of the Galilean narrative and parables.[1]

Sherwin-White goes on to say that "the narrative . . . coheres beautifully." The Gospels and Acts, therefore, take their place as historical documents which arose from, and also illustrate, a particular period.

We have claimed that Christian sources are as valuable as non-Christian sources for our knowledge of history. Can that be demonstrated? Let us investigate the seventy-year period 6 B.C. to A.D. 60, which encompasses the life of Jesus and the first generation of his followers. It will be noticed from what follows that there are a number of points at which Christian and non-Christian sources "intersect." For example, both sets of sources indicate that Archelaus succeeded Herod as ruler of Judea and that subsequently, when Quirinius was governor of Syria, the people of Judea were subjected to a form of personal taxation levied by the Romans.

As you compare the two sets of information you will notice that the Christian sources are as detailed and careful as the non-Christian sources. Christian sources contribute, on an equal footing with non-Christian sources, pieces of information that form part of the fabric of known history. In matters of historical detail, the Christian writers are as valuable to the historian as the non-Christian.

What is the point of these comparisons? Just this: if at the point of "intersection" the Christian evidence about kings, governors and other important people is proved reliable by the non-Christian evidence, should we not also

accept Christian evidence about lesser persons as reliable even though there
is no "intersecting" non-Christian evidence? To be consistent we will be prepared to accept Jairus, Joseph of Arimathaea and Nicodemus, to mention
just three, as genuine figures of history although, through lack of notoriety
or fame, they were unrecorded in secular sources.

How can we be sure of the historicity of an event or person in antiquity?
One historical source may be sufficient to inspire confidence, especially if,
at points where he can be checked, the writer proves trustworthy. But if we
have more than one source, and if they are independent, the ground becomes firmer.

History textbooks tell us that a major war occurred in Palestine in A.D.
66-70 between the Jews and the Romans. But did it in fact happen? How do
the authors of the textbooks know? How can we know?

In Josephus's *Jewish War* we have a major and detailed written history of
the conflict. But in addition we have some information from Tacitus (A.D.
55-c. 120), Suetonius (A.D. 69-c. 140) and Dio Cassius (A.D. 150 to early
third century). There are also some coins minted by the Jewish revolutionaries, as well as the archaeological finds at Masada where one of the factions
underwent Roman siege. Certainly there are some loose ends, some discrepancies—that is the nature of primary sources—but there can be no doubt
that the war took place.

Similarly, how can we know that Jesus of Nazareth was a genuine figure
of history? The method of inquiry is exactly the same in principle as for establishing the reality of the Jewish War. In the case of Jesus we have not one
source but many. Most, to be sure, are favorable, but some are neutral, while
others are hostile.

Let us summarize some of the ways in which we are able to objectively
crosscheck historical data from source to source with respect to Jesus and
Christian origins.

1. Non-Christian writers like Tacitus and Josephus tell us that Jesus was
a historical figure who was executed in Judea sometime between A.D. 26 and
36; Pliny informs us that he was subsequently worshipped as a god. The
non-Christian sources tell us the Christian movement spread to many places
including Rome by A.D. 50 or earlier.

2. The data in the Acts and Paul's letters when crosschecked against political inscriptions and other sources indicate that Paul's letters were written in the period A.D. 50-65. These dates are accurate to within a year or two of this time frame.

3. Leaders of the early church like Clement, Ignatius and Polycarp, who wrote late in the first and early in the second centuries, quote extensively from almost every New Testament scroll, thus establishing their existence and use by c. 100 at the latest. Paul's letters are obviously much earlier and perhaps other parts are as well. The literature of the New Testament was written closer in time to Jesus than many ancient writings are to the events or persons they describe.

4. The rapid spread of Christianity throughout the Greek-speaking world and from there to Latin, Syriac and Coptic-speaking areas together with the accompanying need for manuscripts for reading in church and the survival of many of these manuscripts means that today we are able scientifically to reconstruct, almost to perfection, the text of the scrolls of the New Testament as they were originally written.

5. The existence of not one but four Gospels gives us many opportunities to crosscheck many of the details about Jesus, the focus figure. For two of the writers, Mark and John, eyewitness claims are made, and we have attempted to show the reasonableness of those claims. The other two, Matthew and Luke, incorporate Mark within their Gospels, a fact which allows us to check their accuracy or their proneness to exaggerate. While neither author slavishly follows Mark, both emerge as sober and careful scribes.

By crosschecking independent author against independent author we can be confident of the details and circumstances of Jesus' birth, the broad outlines and nature of his activities in Galilee and Judea, the circumstances of his betrayal and execution, as well as those of his resurrection. However, only in a broad-brush sense can a "life of Jesus" be reconstructed from the sources, since they are Gospels and not biographies in the modern sense. They were each written to present and proclaim Jesus, not to become objects of historical research. That they are such, and to a significant degree, is incidental to their primary function.

6. Luke-Acts and John, which were written independently, both refer to the historic coming of the Holy Spirit soon after the ministry of Jesus. John's Gospel is written in such a way as to presume this event (for example, Jn 7:39), whereas Luke wrote specifically to describe when and how it happened (Acts 2:1-4; 11:16-17).

7. Paul's letters and the Acts of the Apostles, which were also written independently, are open to crosschecking at a number of points. By this means we can be confident of the existence and the leadership of the Jerusalem church (Acts 1—7; Gal 1:18—2:9). The same sources, when crosschecked, establish the historic spread of Christianity to the Gentile world, including Rome itself (Acts 28:16; Phil 1:13; 4:22), a point that Tacitus also corroborates (*Annals* 15.44:2-8).

At many points of historical importance about Jesus and Christian beginnings we have not one but several independent sources, not all of them sympathetic to Jesus. If we accept the historicity of the Jewish War on the grounds of independent sources that are able to be crosschecked it is inconsistent to doubt the essential historicity of Jesus and the early church.

APPENDIX: INTERSECTIONS

Date	Event	Biblical Source	Extrabiblical Source
6 B.C.	King Herod and the killing of the boys	Then Herod . . . sent and killed all the male children in Bethlehem and in all that region who were two years old or under . . . (Mt 2:16)	When [Augustus] heard that Herod king of the Jews had ordered all the boys in Syria under the age of two to be put to death and that the king's son was among those killed, he said, "I'd rather be Herod's pig than Herod's son." (Macrobius *Saturnalia* 2.4.11)

Date	Event	Biblical Source	Extrabiblical Source
4 B.C.	Archelaus ruler of Judea	When he [Joseph] heard that Archelaus reigned over Judea in place of his father Herod . . . (Mt 2:22)	[Augustus] gave half the kingdom to Archelaus with the title of ethnarch. (Josephus *Jewish War* 2.94)
A.D. 6, 7	Roman annexation and assessment	The . . . enrollment, when Quirinius was governor of Syria . . . (Lk 2:2)	The territory subject to Archelaus was added to Syria and Quirinius . . . was sent by Caesar to take a census of property in Syria and to sell the Estate of Archelaus. (Josephus *Jewish Antiquities* 17.355)
A.D. 6, 7	The revolt of Judas	Judas the Galilean arose in the days of the census. (Acts 5:37)	The territory of Archelaus was now reduced to a province. . . . [A] Galilean . . . Judas incited his countrymen to revolt . . . [over] paying tribute to the Romans. (*Jewish War* 2.118)
A.D. 28	Emperor, prefect, high priest	In the fifteenth year . . . of Tiberius Caesar, Pontius Pilate being governor of Judea . . . in the high-priesthood of Annas and Caiaphas, the word of God came to John. (Lk 3:1-2)	Pilate being sent by Tiberius as procurator to Judaea (*Jewish War* 2.169). Herod put [John the Baptist] to death, though he was a good man. (*Jewish Antiquities* 18.113-117)

Date	Event	Biblical Source	Extrabiblical Source
A.D. 33	Execution of Jesus	So Pilate . . . delivered him [Jesus] to be crucified. (Mk 15:15)	Christus . . . suffered the exteme penalty . . . at the hands of . . . Pontius Pilate. (Tacitus Annals 15.44)
A.D. c. 36	Aretus IV (9 B.C. - A.D. 40), king of the Nabateans	At Damascus, the governor under King Aretas guarded the city of Damascus in order to seize me. (2 Cor 11:32)	A quarrel . . . arose between Aretas king of Petra, and Herod [Antipas] [who] had taken the daughter of Aretas as his wife. (Jewish Antiquities 18.109)
A.D. 44	Death of Agrippa I	The people of Tyre and Sidon . . . came to him in a body, and . . . asked for peace . . . Herod put on his royal robes, took his seat upon the throne, and made an oration to them. And the people shouted "The voice of a god, and not of a man!" Immediately an angel of the Lord smote him, because he did not give God the glory. (Acts 12:20-23)	Clad in a garment woven completely of silver . . . he entered the theatre at daybreak. There the silver, illuminated by the touch of the first rays of the sun . . . inspired awe . . . [H]is flatterers addressed him as a god . . . [T]he king did not rebuke him . . . felt a stab of pain in his heart . . . [A]fter five days . . . he departed this life. (Jewish Antiquities 19.344-349)
A.D. 45-46	Famine	Agabus . . . foretold . . . a great famine over all the world; and this took place in the days of Claudius. (Acts 11:28)	It was in the administration of Tiberius Alexander that the great famine occurred in Judaea. (Jewish Antiquities 20.101)

Date	Event	Biblical Source	Extrabiblical Source
A.D. 49	Claudius's expulsion of Jews from Rome	And he [Paul] found a Jew named Aquila, a native of Pontus, lately come from Italy with his wife Priscilla, because Claudius had commanded all the Jews to leave Rome. (Acts 18:2)	Since the Jews constantly made disturbances at the instigation of Chrestus, he [Claudius] expelled them from Rome. (Suetonius, *Life of Claudius* 25.4)
A.D. 51	Gallio, proconsul of Achaia	But when Gallio was proconsul of Achaia . . . (Acts 18:2)	See the inscription at Delphi which fixed Gallio's appointment at (July) c. A.D. 51.
c. A.D. 57	James the brother of Jesus	When we had come to Jerusalem . . . Paul went with us to James; and all the elders were present. (Acts 21:17-18)	c. A.D. 62 Death of Festus . . . Caesar sent Albinus. . . . The king removed Joseph from high priesthood . . . bestowed the succession on the son of Ananus, likewise called . . . Ananus . . . convened the judges of the Sanhedrin and brought before them . . . James, the brother of Jesus who was called the Christ . . . to be stoned. (*Jewish Antiquities* 20.200)

Date	Event	Biblical Source	Extrabiblical Source
c. A.D. 57	The Egyptian prophet	Are you not the Egyptian, then, who recently stirred up a revolt and led the four thousand men of the assassins out into the wilderness? (Acts 21:38)	The Egyptian false prophet . . . appeared in the country, collected a following of about thirty thousand dupes, and led them . . . from the desert to the . . . mount of Olives. (Jewish War 2.261)
c. A.D. 47	Ananias the high priest	And the high priest Ananias commanded those who stood by him to strike him [Paul] on the mouth. (Acts 23:2, cf. 24:1)	Herod King of Chalcis now removed Joseph, the son of Camei, from the high priesthood and assigned the office to Ananias, son of Nebedaios, as successor. (Jewish Antiquities 20.103)
c. A.D. 52	Felix, Roman procurator (A.D. 52-60) and Drusilla	Felix . . . with his wife Drusilla, who was a Jewess . . . sent for Paul and heard him speak upon faith in Christ Jesus. (Acts 24:24)	At the time when Felix was procurator of Judaea [Drusilla] . . . marr[ied] Felix. (Jewish Antiquities 20.131-143; cf. Tacitus History 5.9; Annals 12.54)
c. A.D. 60	Festus, Roman procurator (A.D. 60-62?)	But when two years had elapsed, Felix was succeeded by Porcius Festus. (Acts 24:27)	When Porcius Festus was sent by Nero as successor to Felix . . . (Jewish Antiquities 20.182)

Date	Event	Biblical Source	Extrabiblical Source
c. A.D. 60	King Agrippa II and Berenice	Now, when some days had passed, Agrippa the king and Bernice arrived at Caesarea to welcome Festus. (Acts 25:13)	After the death of Herod [King of Chalcis] who had been her uncle and husband, Bernice lived for a long time as a widow. But when the report gained currency that she had a liaison with her brother [Agrippa] she induced Polemo king of Cilicia to be circumcised and to take her in marriage. (*Jewish Antiquities* 20.145)

FURTHER READING

I. Howard Marshall, *I Believe in the Historical Jesus* (Grand Rapids: Eerdmans, 1977).

John A. T. Robinson, *Can We Trust the New Testament?* (Grand Rapids: Eerdmans, 1977).

17

WHO IS JESUS?

Whatever your opinion of Jesus there is little doubt that you will have some knowledge of who he was and what happened to him. It is remarkable that he has had, and continues to have, such an impact on people and on history. Unlike ben Kosiba, who died a century later and to whom we have referred already, Jesus wrote no letters, led no armies, minted no coins and issued no land deeds. Yet few have heard of ben Kosiba, whereas Jesus is well known. Why?

Ben Kosiba enjoyed a tremendous following for three or so years. More than half a million men were prepared to die for the cause he led, including the pathetic remnants of his forces whom the Romans starved to death in the caves of the bleak desert ravines near the Dead Sea. Such was their loyalty to him that his various letters were carefully bound together and buried in the cave for safekeeping, only to be recovered in the twentieth century. And yet he is as obscure a figure to us as Judas the Galilean, Barabbas or Simon bar Gioras, to mention only a few of the dozen prominent revolutionary leaders who arose in that general period but who are forgotten today.

Jesus continues to hold a strange fascination even for many outside the circle of Christian belief and church membership. Movies continue to be made about him, rock operas composed and outlandish alternative theories put forward.

This is not to imply that Jesus was obscure then, only to become famous later—a kind of reverse ben Kosiba. Jesus had a tremendous impact on events and people in his own generation. The New Testament, whose trustworthiness is the subject of this book, is the tangible evidence of that impact. It is not one document but twenty-seven separate pieces of literature written by nine or ten different authors, most of whom wrote without reference to, or knowledge of, what the others had written.

By contrast, it does not seem that even one person felt moved to write about ben Kosiba immediately after his death,[1] although during his lifetime Rabbi Akiba had hailed him as Messiah, the fulfillment of the long-expected star of Jacob who would rule the world (Num 24:17). For this reason he was known by some as bar Kokhba, which means "son of a star," or "Messiah." For others, however, he came to have a different name. After his death, when so many hopes and dreams were smashed, his name was subtly altered by some to ben Koziba, "son of a liar." Notice the sequence—ben Kosiba, bar Kokhba, ben Koziba, oblivion.

Not so with Jesus. Within a few years of his lifetime, nine or ten independent writers had recorded their testimony for all to read. This is to state the numbers conservatively, since as we have seen, buried within Matthew and Luke are the written (or oral) sources Q, L, M and perhaps others as well. Thus we have a dozen independent writers, each of whom presents the same exalted view of Jesus. In a criminal trial such unity of independent testimony would certainly persuade a judge and jury that what is said is the truth. For my part this analogy holds good for the writers and source strands that make up the New Testament.

But why did ben Kosiba pass out of memory whereas Jesus created such an impact? It was, in part, that ben Kosiba failed to defeat the Romans. Further, his period in public life was brief. Oblivion, or relative oblivion, was to be his lot. And the reason? After ben Kosiba died, memory of him died with those who knew him.

Jesus, however, lived on in the memory of his generation and in each generation after. This was not only because of his ethical teachings or his reformist insights into contemporary Jewish society. If this had been all there was to it, it is unlikely that Jesus would have survived a century or two in the memories of those who came after him. Ethics and the principles for the reform of society were present in what Jesus said and did, but they are not at the center. Reduced to the barest essentials, Jesus' "message" was that God himself would soon come into human affairs to establish his kingdom of justice, goodness and peace, and that God was already doing this in the person of Jesus.

As the Son of God, at that very time as well as at the end, Jesus was the bearer of the kingdom of God in a world corrupted by forces opposite to God's character and purpose. These startling claims of Jesus (imagine if someone said them today) were by no means empty. Demons were cast out, the deaf given their hearing, the blind their sight, the dumb their speech, the sick their health and the dead their life as visible "signs" of the truth of Jesus' words that the kingdom was and would be present in him. The great and crowning sign that Jesus spoke the truth was that God raised him to life on the third day after his execution by the Romans.

Put simply, the reason Jesus lived and lives subjectively in the memory of his followers is that he lived and lives *objectively* after three days in the tomb. What Jesus said about God's intentions for mankind and what he said about himself as the One who carried out those intentions as God's Son, is confirmed and established by his resurrection from the dead.

Without the resurrection, Jesus becomes just another prophet whose prophecies came to nothing, another mistaken dreamer, another idealistic reformer. Indeed this is all Jesus was if the resurrection did not take place.

That Jesus can never be viewed primarily as a teacher of ethics or as a reformer of society is quite clear from Paul's words, "If for this life only we have hoped in Christ, we [Christians] are of all men most to be pitied" (1 Cor 15:19). Paul continues immediately, "But in fact Christ has been raised from the dead," something he and his fellow New Testament writers repeatedly say and universally assume. The resurrection is inextricably part of the fabric of the New Testament; destroy it or remove it and the New Testament becomes an unreliable bundle of rags and tatters.

What I am attempting to establish is that a Jesus who died (c. 33) as no more than a teacher and reformer would have been as little known, or almost as little known, as ben Kosiba, who died a century later.

Consider some words the apostle Paul wrote to a group of people in faraway Macedonia no more than seventeen years after the execution of Jesus:

You turned to God from idols, to serve a living and true God, and to

wait for his Son from heaven, whom he raised from the dead. (1 Thess
1:9-10)

Fundamental to what Paul told the Thessalonians was that Jesus was God's
Son and that God had raised him from the dead. The act of receiving these
pieces of information established the Thessalonians as Christian believers.

The question is: was Paul's communication to them true or false? If it was
false, either Paul was somehow deceived or he was a deliberate deceiver of
others. Few people reading Paul would accept the latter view, though the
former is certainly possible. To return to the courtroom analogy, Paul is only
one of the witnesses—one witness among a dozen or so. If all the witnesses,
independently of each other, state that Jesus was the Son of God and that he
was raised from the dead, as they do, what then? I can only ask the reader
to be a member of the jury and arrive at his own verdict. For my part the
evidence is clear and compelling.

The logic is simple. People became Christians then on the basis of information they were given about Jesus. The critical questions are: was the information true or untrue? Did the information correspond with, and give expression to, reality or not? The information is an *effect* for which there was a
cause, like a ripple caused by a stone thrown into a pond. What *caused* the
effect? Was it the stone thrown into the pond as the bystanders said, or was
it something else? Was Jesus in reality the Son of God raised from the dead,
as the witnesses said, or were these only words that had no basis in fact? But
if what purports to be the cause—the deity and resurrection of Jesus—was
not the cause, what was? The writers must all have been either deceived or
cold-blooded deceivers.

Those are the questions that I have turned over and over in my mind and
looked at from different angles. Philosophically and scientifically there are
problems with a resurrection, and I feel those as keenly as most. But I cannot
escape the historical question. Did the resurrection happen or not? If it happened, it happened—and so much the worse for my dogmas. I certainly will
not be able to regard Jesus with the indifference with which I might view ben
Kosiba.

But at that point the questions about Jesus stop, or at least slow down,
and the questions about me begin.

FURTHER READING

William Lane Craig, "The Empty Tomb of Jesus," *Gospel Perspectives*, ed. R. T. France and David Wenham, vol. 2 (Sheffield: JSOT Press, 1981).

George Eldon Ladd, *I Believe in the Resurrection of Jesus* (Grand Rapids: Eerdmans, 1975).

C. F. D. Moule, *The Phenomenon of the New Testament* (London: SCM Press, 1968).

18

Historical Origins of Christianity and Islam

Due to heightened interest in Islam any discussion about the origins of Christianity inevitably prompts questions about the origins of Islam.

Jesus Christ and Muhammad

Jesus Christ and Muhammad were genuine figures of history. Christianity arose from Christ, and Islam from Muhammad. A sacred text issued from the work of each—the New Testament from Christ, the Qur'an from Muhammad.

We need to be clear about dates and places. Jesus, a Jew, was born in Bethlehem c. 6 B.C. and died in Jerusalem A.D. 33.[1] According to the New Testament, Jesus was the Messiah, the Son of God who had been conceived in the womb of Mary by direct intervention of God. His many miracles were evidence of his deity. Within three days of his death by crucifixion he was raised alive from the dead.

Muhammad ibn Abdullah, an Arab, was born in Mecca in c. A.D. 570 and died in Medina in A.D. 632. An orphan from his early years, Muhammad traveled extensively throughout the Arabian peninsula. In his fortieth year Muhammad received and began to articulate the oracles of Allah. ("Allah," derived from *al-ilah*, means "*the* God," that is, the one and only God). Muhammad left Mecca, where he was subjected to persecution, for Medina, where he became dominant. Subsequently he returned to Mecca in triumph. According to Islamic belief Muhammad was the last of God's prophets.

Christians worship Jesus as Son of God, as Emmanuel "God with us" who is equal in deity as God the Father, a belief the Qur'an repudiates (see below). For Muslims Muhammad is the Prophet of Allah, a perfect believer, the man to emulate as leader and statesman.

NAMES OF TEXTS: THE "NEW TESTAMENT" AND THE "QUR'AN"

The names of the texts are significant.

The "*New* Testament" is so called because it connects with and completes the "*Old* Testament." Together these "testaments" comprise the Bible; neither testament stands alone. Both point to Christ, the Old Testament prophesying him beforehand, the New Testament proclaiming him afterward.

Jesus and the apostles were steeped in the Old Testament and quote it repeatedly to show that its prophetic message has been fulfilled and realized in Jesus, Messiah and Son of God.

The word *Qur'an* means the "recital," because the angel Gabriel instructed Muhammad to "*recite* in the name of your Lord, who created man."

JUDAISM AND CHRISTIANITY IN THE QUR'AN

Whereas the New Testament flows out of the Old Testament, the prophet Muhammad "recites" teachings drawn from a range of sources, including Jewish and Christian traditions. These, however, are not based directly on the Old Testament and the New Testament but rather indirectly on stories then in circulation about Old Testament figures like Abraham and Moses and New Testament figures like Mary and Jesus. These are so different from the Bible's accounts that they must have come from different tradition streams. Rarely, if ever, does the Qur'an exactly quote the texts of the New or the Old Testament.[2]

The ultimate sources of these traditions are unclear. Some Jewish references appear to come through the filter of stories from the Talmud (sixth century) while some Christian references appear to have originated from the Apocryphal Gospels (third to fifth centuries).

Versions of Jewish and Christian beliefs were current among Arabs in the era when Muhammad began to teach. For example, trinitarian belief among some Syrian Christians at that time pointed not to the Father, the Son and the Holy Spirit but to Jesus, Mary and God the Father. This would explain the Qur'an's insistence on Allah as the only God:

> O people of the Book [= Christians] . . . do not say anything but the truth about Allah. The Messiah, Jesus the son of Mary, was no more than Allah's messenger and his Word, which he sent forth into Mary, a spirit proceeding from him. So believe in Allah and his messengers, but do not say, "Three." Refrain and it will be better for you. Allah is but one God; far be it for him to have a son. (Sura 4:169-172)

Muhammad's monotheism appears to be in reaction against a distorted and heretical form of trinitarian belief. The Orthodox churches, which exist side by side with Islam in the Middle East, are dominated by images of Mary holding her baby son. In these circumstances Muslim insistence on monotheism is understandable.

The insistence "far be it for [Allah] to have a son" also appears as "Far be it from Allah that he should *beget* a son! When he decrees that something shall be, he has only to say, 'Be!'—and it is" (Sura 19:36). The New Testament, however, does not teach that God is the *biological* "father" of Jesus. Muhammad may be correcting a crass understanding of New Testament teaching current at that time.

JESUS IN THE QUR'AN

According to the Qur'an Mary conceived the Messiah, Jesus, by the direct intervention of Allah. The angels said,

> "Mary, Allah bids you rejoice in a Word from himself, in him who is called the Messiah, Jesus son of Mary. He is eminent in this world and the next, one of those brought near to him. He will speak to men in the cradle and as a full-grown man; he will be one of the upright."
>
> "My Lord," said Mary, "how shall I have a child? No man has ever touched me."
>
> "So shall it be," was the reply; "Allah creates whom he pleases. Whatever he decrees he simply says 'Be!'—and it is.
>
> "Allah will instruct him in the Book and in wisdom, in the Law and the Gospel; he will be a messenger to the Israelites. He will say, 'I come

to you with a sign from your Lord. I will create for you from clay the
form of a bird; I will breath into it and by Allah's permission it will become a real bird.'"

Jesus will be sent as messenger to Israel. The creation of a bird from
clay is found in the *Infancy Gospel of Thomas*, a second-century apocryphal work.

Another example of the Qur'an's dependence on post-New Testament
teaching is its denial of Jesus' death.

> The people of the book [here = the Jews] refused the truth and uttered
> a great slander against Mary [attributing her pregnancy to immoral-
> ity]. They said, "We have killed the Messiah, Jesus son of Mary, the
> messenger of Allah."
>
> But they did not kill him, they did not crucify him; it only seemed
> to them to be so. . . . In fact Allah raised him to himself . . . on the day
> of resurrection he shall witness against them. (Sura 4:155-157)[3]

The words, "it only *seemed* to them to be so" appear to follow an errone-
ous doctrine known as "Docetism," based on the Greek word for "to seem,"
or "appear."[4] Docetism, an early version of Gnosticism, asserted that Jesus
only "seemed" to be human, that he only "seemed" to die and that he only
"seemed" to have been raised *bodily*.

Since denial of Jesus' crucifixion is so firmly part of Muslim theology, its
narration in the Gospels is held to be proof positive of their inaccuracy.

HISTORICAL EVIDENCE FOR JESUS AND MUHAMMAD

Amount of time between text and person. The biographies of Jesus were
written within a lifetime of his lifetime. An early Gospel (Mark's) was written
within forty years of Jesus' lifespan, based on his memorized teachings and
perhaps on words copied down by scribes.

All four Gospels and the remainder of the New Testament were completed within about half a century of Jesus, except the Revelation (written c.
A.D. 95).

There are three main sources for the life and teaching of Muhammad: the
Qur'an, the earliest biographies and the Tradition (the Hadith).

The Qur'an as we have it originated with one of Muhammad's companions, Zaid ibn Thabit. Soon after Muhammad's death Zaid compiled the teachings of the Prophet based on collections of his words copied by scribes or teachings memorized by his hearers. Other codices were circulating among the Arabic tribes including ones by another companion Abdullah ibn Mas'ud, said by some authorities to be a superior compilation.[5] It appears that there were various textual differences between Zaid's and Masud's versions.[6]

Twenty years after Muhammad's death, under Uthman (the third Caliph), Zaid's version was nominated as the official version, with other compilations suppressed, including Masud's. The new "official" version was not written by Zaid (whose version was in his local dialect) but dictated by him to Sa'id ibn al-'As, an expert in classical Arabic.[7] Despite the destruction of other codices the Zaid version is most likely a true account of the revelations to the Prophet.

The earliest biography of Muhammad, the *Sira* by Ibn Ishaq, was not completed until a century and a half after Muhammad's death. This biography, however, did not survive in its own right, but only within Ibn Hisham's biography written 213 years after the death of Muhammad.

This means that the available biography of Muhammad was written from the perspective of an Islam that by then was well established. (By analogy, this would be like the Gospels being written after the Apostles' Creed had been formulated, two hundred years after Jesus. The opposite, however, was the case. The Christian Creed was formulated in the light of the Gospel, not vice versa.)

The Traditions of the Prophet (Hadith) have almost equal authority with the Qur'an. The earliest extant Hadith dates from the eighth century.

The teaching of Muhammad in the Qur'an and biographical information in the Sira and the Hadith are separate entities and the forms in which they now exist postdate the Prophet by several centuries.

Thus while the teachings of the Prophet in the Qur'an in the Zaid text is close to the time of the Prophet's death, the biographical sources in the Sira and the Hadith are later by several centuries.

The problem of accessibility to the origins of Islam is well summarized by Patricia Crone and Michael Cook:

The tradition which places this . . . revelation in its historical context is not attested before the middle of the eighth [century]. The historicity of the Islamic tradition is thus to some degree problematic.[8]

Historically, therefore, the origins of Christianity and Islam are of quite a different order. Unlike the Qur'an the Gospels are at the same time biographies of Jesus *and* accounts of his teachings. His immediate followers continued to serve him after his life span and were responsible directly or indirectly for the production of the Gospels that appeared within the next half-century.

Recovery of the biographical outline. A biographical outline of Jesus' ministry and also the history of earliest Christianity is historically recoverable. This is due first to the closeness of the texts to the events and second to the intrinsically historical and geographical character of the texts. Furthermore, the Roman historian Tacitus, who was unsympathetic to Christians, gives his own independent "broad-brush" account of the origin of Christianity that confirms the New Testament outline (*Annals* 15.44).[9]

No such confidence is possible in recovering a life story of Muhammad.

Comparison with the original. As noted above, because the Qur'an was subjected to several standardizing recensions it means that we cannot easily get back beyond these to the mind of the Prophet.

The New Testament was also subjected to a standardizing procedure in late antiquity creating a uniform text that was later known as the "Textus Receptus." From the nineteenth century, however, numerous early texts of the New Testament have been discovered that had escaped standardization. From that time the science of textual criticism developed. Due to the plethora of texts and the diligence of textual critics we are able to establish a text of the New Testament that is very close to the words written by the original authors.

Here, then, is a major difference between the documentation of Christianity and Islam. In the case of Jesus, his life and teaching are recorded close to him and we have the texts as they left the hands of Matthew and the other Gospel writers. In regard to Muhammad, however, though his teachings were written down soon after his death, no text from his time survives, only later standardized versions.[10]

Furthermore, the earliest extant account of his life is two centuries later and is likely colored by Islamic beliefs that had by then become "official."

Issues relating to Christianity and Islam are deeply sensitive. The reader must judge the relative strength of historical evidence for Jesus and the rise of Christianity and Muhammad and the rise of Islam.

Based on the number of sources, their concrete character, their linkages with world history and above all their closeness in time to their subject there can be no doubt that the historical basis for Jesus and the contemporary belief in him as Son of God are historically formidable.

DIFFERENT KINDS OF LITERATURE

The number of different kinds. The New Testament consists of three different kinds of literature—Gospels, Acts and Letters—each of which is historical and geographical in character. The Gospels place Jesus in a real historical and geographical context, naming Jewish rulers, Roman emperors and governors, as well as numerous towns and cities. Likewise the book of Acts narrates its history with many connecting historical and geographical linkages. The Letters also are historical, written by named authors to named readers in known locations with identifiable circumstances.

By contrast, the Qur'an consists only of oracles from God spoken to Muhammad and gives little idea of the times when or the places where Muhammad received the revelations. There are no linkages to wider world history. Only a few of Muhammad's contemporaries are mentioned.

The arrangements of the texts. The New Testament texts are arranged in logical historical sequence beginning with the four biographies of Jesus, followed by the book of Acts narrating the spread of earliest Christianity. Only then do we meet the Letters setting out doctrinal beliefs. Appropriately the New Testament ends with the Revelation, a book that sets out a vision of the ultimate future. Christians of early centuries arranged these texts in this historical sequence due to their conviction that "the word became flesh and dwelt among us," that is, that the Son of God had come at a particular time and place and that the impact of his coming continues.

The Qur'an, however, is a sequence of unconnected oracles that stand free of any historical or geographical setting. Indeed, it is a matter of debate by scholars as to the right historical sequence in which the oracles should be arranged in the Qur'an. The oldest Arabic texts followed no historical sequence for the Suras (chapters) but were arranged according to length, the longest first. Some English translations have attempted to locate the oracles in a reconstructed historical order while others begin with the briefer, more poetic revelations to Muhammad.[11]

The sequence of the oracles is important since Muhammad's experience in Mecca (when persecuted) differs from that in Medina (when dominant). Some teachings appear to be in conflict, for example, regarding the use of compulsion in religion. Sura 2:256 enjoins, "Let there be no compulsion in religion" whereas Sura 9:5 urges, "fight and slay the pagans wherever you find them." Some Muslim scholars give precedence to the "Sword Verse" (Sura 9:5) since it was given in Medina near the end of the Prophet's life. The resolution of conflicting texts is called abrogation.

The number of authors. The New Testament is a collection of twenty-seven separate texts, written in Greek by nine authors expressed in distinctive styles and with varying emphases.

By contrast, the Qur'an is written in classical Arabic and is more or less uniform throughout, the product of one mind.

The concreteness of the text. The Qur'an is entirely "didactic." Allah is the speaker throughout so that the Qur'an is literally his word, spoken to and thus through his Prophet.

On the other hand, the teachings of Jesus in the Gospels and the apostles in the Letters, which are often connected to a historical and geographical setting, are "concrete" in character. Often there is a known context for the teaching of the Lord and his apostles.

READING THE NEW TESTAMENT

The different styles of literature evoke different styles of interpretation.

The Qur'an's rather freestanding "doctrinal" content invites a more direct and immediate interpretation. The word *Islam* means "submission," that is, to the will of Allah, as expressed to his Prophet and articulated in the Qur'an.

It was not that the Prophet himself was inspired. The origin of truth is Allah and the Tablet preserved in heaven (Sura 85:22). There had been earlier revelations—to Moses and David (for Jews), to Jesus (for Gentiles). Finally Allah revealed his will to Muhammad (for Arabs and ultimately to all people). For Muslims, therefore, the Qur'an is inspired in an absolute, non-negotiable sense.

New Testament writers, on the other hand, are conscious of their own human involvement in their texts. True, they envisage their texts about Jesus as completing the Old Testament, that is, as "Holy Writing" or "Scripture." Thus the writings of the New Testament are at the same time divine and human, the work of the Spirit of God in and through genuinely human authors. This emerges, for example, in some words written by the apostle Paul to the wayward Corinthians, "what *I* am writing to you is a command of *the Lord*" (1 Cor 14:37, italics mine).

Reading New Testament texts calls for sensitivity to the original context and intention of writers like John or Paul ("authorial intent"). The prior question is, What did the author intend his original readers to believe or do in that situation? When John wrote, "these [signs that Jesus did] are written that you may believe that Jesus is the Christ, the Son of God" (Jn 20:31), his intention for the original readers—and all other readers since—is straight-forward. When, however, Paul calls for wives to wear a marriage veil when prophesying (1 Cor 11:5), the modern reader has to work a little harder and ask the questions: (1) Why did Paul write this then? (2) Is there a principle to be discovered here? (3) How does this principle apply today? How does this principle apply now? In both John 20:31 and 1 Corinthians 11:5 answers are forthcoming from the respective contexts.

In other words, for the reader of the New Testament there is a principle of "submission" to God through the scriptural text. It is not a "blind," unthinking submission but one in which the mind has been fully (and prayerfully) engaged in the intention and meaning of the scriptural text. That text, however, will not be studied in isolation but in relation to the message of the Bible globally.

Biblical scholarship calls for reverence and genuine devotion to God. But it is also "scientific" in the sense that identifiable skills and disciplines are involved, for example, in the languages of the Bible and the history of its times. In this regard, biblical scholarship is not unrelated to scholarship in ancient Near Eastern and Graeco-Roman fields of study.

THE SON OF GOD AND THE PROPHET

Muhammad arose at a time when Arab tribes were caught up in a monotheism debased by idolatry and superstition. Most likely the versions of Christianity he encountered were not true to the New Testament but had been corrupted through the passage of time. Furthermore, he perceived Christianity as plagued by numerous factions. He saw himself as the final prophet of the monotheism of Abraham and Jesus as a lesser precursor.

Nothing could be further from the truth according to the New Testament. The opening words of the letter to the Hebrews states, "In many and various ways God spoke of old to our fathers by the prophets; but *in these last days* he has spoken to us by a Son." The passage continues, stating that "Son" to be "God," whom angels worship and serve. Paul teaches that the fullness of deity dwelt bodily in Jesus Christ (Col 2:9).

In Islamic theology Jesus was a lesser prophet superseded by Muhammad the Prophet. In starkest contrast with this view of him the New Testament insists on the uniqueness and the finality of Jesus, the Son of God. The Greek word *hapax*, meaning "once and for all," is repeatedly applied to him (for example, 1 Pet 3:18 "Christ . . . died for sins *once for all,* the righteous for the unrighteous, that he might bring us to God"). Jesus Christ is the Lord and Savior of all people, the one mediator between God and man (1 Tim 2:5). This Jesus is "the way [to God], and the truth, and the life" for all peoples (Jn 14:6).

This is the message of the New Testament, its "glad tidings." It is a message that is credible based on the breadth of numbers of witnesses who testify to it, the historical reliability of its texts, their chronological closeness to Jesus and the security of their transmission throughout the intervening years.

NOTES

Chapter 1: Introduction: Is There History?
[1]Antony Beevor, *The Fall of Berlin 1945* (New York: Viking, 2002).

Chapter 2: The Question of Truth
[1]See, for example, 2 Pet 1:16, "We did not follow cleverly devised myths . . ."
[2]See I. Howard Marshall, *Biblical Inspiration* (Grand Rapids: Eerdmans, 1982).
[3]F. F. Bruce, *The New Testament Documents* (Leicester, U.K.: Inter-Varsity Press, 1963).

Chapter 3: Did Jesus Exist? Early Non-Christian Sources
[1]*Epistles* 10.96, quoted in James Stevenson, ed., *A New Eusebius* (London: SPCK, 1960), p. 14.
[2]See further Stevenson, *New Eusebius,* pp. 7-8.
[3]*Benediction Twelve,* quoted in C. K. Barrett, *The New Testament Background* (London: SPCK, 1961), p. 167.
[4]Yigael Yadin, *Bar-Kokhba* (London: Random House, 1971), p. 137.
[5]Quoted in Eusebius, *Ecclesiastical History,* trans. Kirsopp Lake, Loeb Classical Library, 2 vols. (London: Heinemann, 1926).

Chapter 4: Fixing the Time Frame
[1]John A. T. Robinson, *Redating the New Testament* (London: SCM Press, 1976).
[2]Joseph Barber Lightfoot, index of scriptural passages in *The Apostolic Fathers* (London: Macmillan, 1885), 3.2:522-23.
[3]Ibid., pp. 520-22.
[4]Alexander Roberts and James Donaldson, eds., *The Ante-Nicene Fathers* (Grand Rapids: Eerdmans, 1956), 1:5-21 (see footnotes).

Chapter 5: Is the Transmission Trustworthy?
[1]The time a trained scribe took to copy the four Gospels has been estimated at six weeks, or about three months for the whole New Testament. See William Barclay, *The Gospels and Acts* (London: SCM Press, 1976), 1:25.
[2]Stephen Neill, *The Interpretation of the New Testament, 1861-1961* (London: Oxford University Press, 1964), p. 78.
[3]Ibid., p. 81.

Chapter 6: The Two Witnesses

[1]"Having an approximately parallel point of view," *World Book Dictionary,* 2nd ed., s.v. "synoptic."

[2]And therefore with neither Matthew's nor Luke's Gospel.

Chapter 7: Witness One: The Disciple Whom Jesus Loved

[1]Quoted in Eusebius, *The History of the Church from Christ to Constantine,* trans. G. A. Williamson (New York: Penguin, 1989).

[2]Although both readings occur in ancient manuscripts, the one translated "go on believing" is to be preferred because it occurs in the earliest manuscript and has good support elsewhere.

[3]See further, F. F. Bruce, *Places They Knew* (London: Ark, 1981), pp. 35-38.

[4]Eric M. Meyers and James F. Strange, *Archaeology, the Rabbis and Early Christianity* (London: SCM Press, 1981), p. 160.

[5]If, as it appears, the time of the arrival of the news to Jesus coincided with the time of Lazarus's death (Jn 11:3, cf. 11:11).

[6]Meyers and Strange, *Archaeology, the Rabbis and Early Christianity,* p. 161.

[7]C. H. Dodd, *Historical Tradition in the Fourth Gospel* (Cambridge: Cambridge University Press, 1963), p. 120.

[8]John A. T. Robinson, *Redating the New Testament* (London: SCM Press, 1976), p. 297. Many scholars, however, regard John 9:22 as evidence that this Gospel arises out of the post-70 milieu.

[9]See Mark 3:18 and parallels.

[10]Jesus committing his mother into the care of "the disciple whom Jesus loved" (Jn 19:26) suggests that Joseph had died by that time.

[11]See Edwin Arthur Judge, *The Social Pattern of the Christian Groups in the First Century* (London: Tyndale, 1960), p. 34.

[12]Günther Bornkamm, *Jesus of Nazareth* (London: Hodder and Stoughton, 1960), p. 14.

[13]See Archibald M. Hunter, *According to John* (London: SCM Press, 1968), pp. 97-98.

[14]Robinson, *Redating the New Testament,* p. 299.

[15]Raymond E. Brown, *The Gospel According to John,* vol. 1 (New York: Doubleday, 1966).

[16]C. K. Barrett, *The Gospel According to St John* (London: SPCK, 1960), p. 114.

Chapter 8: Witness Two: Peter Through Mark

[1]William Barclay, *The Gospels and Acts,* vol. 1 (London: SCM Press, 1976), p. 116.

[2]*Histories* 5.9. Antipas is not actually mentioned by name.

[3]See further Harold Hoehner, *Herod Antipas* (Grand Rapids: Eerdmans, 1980), pp. 131-36.

[4]Ibid., pp. 331-42.

[5]Ibid., pp. 317-30.

[6]For discussion about the discovery of the house of Peter in Capernaum see Eric M. Meyers and James F. Strange, *Archaeology, the Rabbis and Early Christianity,* (London: SCM Press, 1981), pp. 59-60, 128-30.

Chapter 9: Luke and Matthew
[1]Quoted in James Stevenson, ed., *A New Eusebius* (London: SPCK, 1957), p. 52.
[2]Ibid.
[3]Ibid.
[4]Edwyn Clement Hoskyns and Francis Noel Davey, *The Riddle of the New Testament* (London: Faber & Faber, n.d.), p. 103.
[5]Ibid.
[6]It is probable, but not certain, that these were written sources. See Archibald M. Hunter, *The Work and Words of Jesus* (London: SCM Press, 1958), where the sources Q, M, L are reproduced separately.
[7]A box containing Scripture verses that was worn on the forehead and arms. See Matthew 23:5.

Chapter 10: The Birth of Jesus
[1]*Time,* December 27, 1976, p. 27.
[2]Macrobius, *The Saturnalia,* trans. Percival Vaughan Davies (New York: Columbia University Press, 1969), p. 171.

Chapter 11: Miracles and the Modern World
[1]Joachim Jeremias, *New Testament Theology,* trans. John Bowden (London: SCM Press, 1971), 1:21.
[2]Ibid., p. 92.
[3]For an exhaustive list of miracles see Reginald Horace Fuller, *Interpreting the Miracles* (London: SCM Press, 1963), pp. 126-27.

Chapter 12: The Resurrection of Jesus
[1]J. Duncan Derrett, *The Anastasis: The Resurrection of Jesus as an Historical Event* (Shipton-on-Stour, U.K.: P. Drinkwater, 1982).
[2]See Justin Martyr *Dialogue with Trypho* 108; and Tertullian *De Spectaculis* 30.
[3]A view associated with Kirsopp Lake, *The Historical Evidence for the Resurrection of Jesus* (New York: Putnam, 1907).
[4]Cf. 1 Corinthians 11:23, "For I received from the Lord what I also delivered to you."
[5]Cf. Acts 13:29. The Gospel of Matthew refers to the burial chamber as *taphos* (27:61, 64, 66; 28:1).
[6]But see John Wenham, *Easter Enigma: Do the Resurrection Stories Contradict One Another?* (Exeter: Paternoster, 1984).
[7]Associated with the views of Ernest Renan, *The Life of Jesus* (New York: H. W. Bell, 1904).

[8]John Shelby Spong, *Resurrection: Myth or Reality?* (San Francisco: HarperSanFrancisco, 1994).

[9]Cited in private correspondence to Josh McDowell.

[10]Quoted in John Stott, *Basic Christianity* (Leicester, U.K.: Inter-Varsity Press, 1974), p. 47.

[11]C. F. D. Moule, *The Phenomenon of the New Testament* (London: SCM Press, 1967), p. 3.

Chapter 13: Paul and the Historical Jesus

[1]Possibly from A.D. 48 if Galatians is Paul's first letter.

[2]Galatians 1:19 perhaps refers to an initial, private consultation. See Acts 9:27-28, where Paul met a wider group in Jerusalem.

[3]The list of resurrection appearances in 1 Corinthians 15:4-8 suggests that they occurred within a limited period of time.

[4]Dale C. Allison, "The Pauline Epistles and the Synoptic Gospels: The Pattern of the Parables," *New Testament Studies*, 28 (1982): 1-32.

[5]David Michael Stanley, *The Apostolic Church in the New Testament* (Westminster, Md.: Newman Press, 1967), pp. 34-37, 364-69.

Chapter 14: The Acts of the Apostles

[1]Acts is addressed to Theophilus, but it is not clear whether he was a real or symbolic person.

[2]See William Barclay, *The Gospels and Acts* (London: SCM Press, 1976), 2:229.

[3]Ernst Haenchen, *The Acts of the Apostles,* trans. Bernard Noble and Gerald Shinn (Oxford: Blackwell, 1971), p. 103, refers to Luke-Acts as "a book of edification."

[4]Jack Finegan, *The Archeology of the New Testament: The Mediterranean World of the Early Christian Apostles* (Boulder, Colo.: Westview Press, 1981), p. 12.

[5]For a summary of the problems of history in Acts see Barclay, *The Gospel and Acts,* pp. 259-81.

[6]Quoted in F. F. Bruce, *The New Testament Documents* (Leicester, U.K.: Inter-Varsity Press, 1979), p. 90.

[7]*Reformed Theological Review* 30 (1971): 7.

[8]A. N. Sherwin-White, *Roman Society and Roman Law in the New Testament* (Oxford: Oxford University Press, 1965).

[9]Colin J. Hemer, "Luke the Historian," *Bulletin of the John Rylands Library* 60 (1977): 36-37.

[10]Martin Hengel, *Acts and the History of Earliest Christianity* (London: SCM Press, 1979), p. 61.

Chapter 16: Is the New Testament Historically Reliable?

[1]A. N. Sherwin-White, *Roman Society and Roman Law in the New Testament,* (Oxford: Oxford University Press, 1965), pp. 138-39.

Chapter 17: Who Is Jesus?
[1]Unless whatever was written has been lost.

Chapter 18: Historical Origins of Christianity and Islam
[1]Most scholars date the crucifixion to A.D. 30. My reason for the later date arises from Luke's statement that John the Baptist began prophesying in A.D. 29 (Lk 3:1-2). This means that Jesus must have commenced his ministry about A.D. 30, hence the A.D. 33 date for the crucifixion.

[2]Sura 21.105 loosely quotes Psalm 37:29.

[3]It is possible Sura 3.54-55 implies Jesus did die.

[4]This is opposed by the noted authority Kenneth Cragg, *Jesus and the Muslim* (London: Allen and Unwin, 1985), p. 173.

[5]John Gilchrist, *Jam' Al-Quran: The Codification of the Qur'an Text* (Warley, U.K.: Rowley Regis, 1989), pp. 60-62.

[6]See ibid., pp. 69-72.

[7]So Ibn Abi Dawud, *Kitab al-Masahif* (Leiden, U.K.: Brill, 1937), p. 22. Also see Leone Caetani, "Uthman and the Recension of the Koran," in *The Origins of the Koran,* ed. Ibn Warraq (New York: Prometheus, 1998), pp. 67-75.

[8]Patricia Crone and Michael Cook, *Hagarism* (Cambridge: Cambridge University Press, 1977), p. 3.

[9]See pp. 25-28 above.

[10]See chapter five above. For transmission of the Qur'an texts see A. Mingara, "The Transmission of the Koran," in *The Origins of the Koran,* ed. Ibn Warraq (New York: Prometheus, 1998), pp. 97-113.

[11]*The Koran,* trans. John Medows Rodwell, Everyman's Library (London: n.p., 1909), is in reconstructed historical order, for example. On the other hand, *The Koran: A New Translation,* trans. N. J. Dawood (Harmondsworth, U.K.: Penguin, 1956), starts with the shorter, more poetic revelations.

Index

Acts of the Apostles, 145-58
  historicity, 153-58
Annas (high priest), 97
Ante-Nicene Fathers, 46
Barnabas, travel to Cyprus, 162
Caiaphas
  in John's Gospel, 64-65
  in Luke's Gospel, 97
  ossuary, 160
Clement, 39, 169
Codex Sinaiticus, 44
Eusebius, 38
Festus (Roman procurator), 37-38
Herod the Great, 100-103, 160
historical data, 168-75
Ignatius (bishop of Antioch), 39-40, 68, 169
Irenaeus, 74, 89, 91
Islam, 181-90
James, 114-16, 159
Jesus
  in Acts, 148
  birth narrative, 98-104
  in Mark's Gospel, 79-88
  miracles, 105-9
  resurrection, 111-34
Jewish sources
  Benediction Twelve, 29-30
  Josephus, 165-66, 170-75
  Pharisees, 30
  Talmud, 30-31
John Mark, 74-77
John the Baptist, 163
John Zebedee, 54-73
Jesus' miracles, 106-8
Jesus' resurrection, 113-14, 118, 128
Joseph, 63

Josephus, 34, 165-66, 168-75
  Jewish Antiquities, 31-34, 171-75
  Jewish War, 12, 34, 45, 171, 174-75
Justin Martyr, 33, 43
Kosiba ben, 16, 33-34, 176-77
L
  miracles, 108-9
  source for Luke's Gospel, 90-92, 96-97
Luke, Gospel of, 89-104
  Acts, 145-58
  agreement with Matthew, 98-100
  history writer, 13-14
  Jesus' miracles, 106-9
  Jesus' resurrection, 129
M
  miracles, 108-9
  source for Matthew's Gospel, 91-94, 96-97
manuscript transmission/translation, 43-47
Mark, Gospel of, 48, 74-88
  Jesus' miracles, 106-9
  Jesus' resurrection, 129
  in Matthew and Luke, 92-97
Matthew, Gospel of, 92-97
  Jesus' miracles, 105-9
  Jesus' resurrection, 129
Muhammad, 181-83
  historical evidence, 184-87
  and Jesus Christ, 190
Muratorian Canon, 89-90, 145
Nathanael, 63
Nicodemus, 64
Papias, 91
Paul (apostle)
  in Acts, 145, 150-52, 156-57
  1 Corinthians, 126-28
  Jesus' resurrection, 111-19
  knowledge of Jesus, 136-44
  letters, 37-38
Peter (apostle), 74-77
  Jesus' resurrection, 114-16
  source for Mark, 74-86
Pharisees, 29
Pliny, 22-25, 27, 34, 43

Polycarp, 39-40
Pompeii, 24-25
Pontius Pilate, 65, 96
Proto-Luke, 90-91, 95
Q
  miracles, 105, 108-9
  source for Matthew and Luke, 91-96
Quirinius, 101
Qumran. 14-15
Qur'an, 182-85
  sources, 186-88
resurrection of Jesus, 111-34
  alternative explanations, 119-26
  appearances, 130-31
  physical, 131-33

"third day" and "first day," 117-19
Suetonius, 28-29, 102, 173
Synoptic Gospels, 48, 69
Tacitus, 25-28, 34, 168, 170, 172, 175
  Annals of Imperial Rome, 14, 25, 45, 172
Talmud, 30-31, 182
time frame
  Jesus' life, 35-37
  non-Pauline letters, 38-42
  Paul's letters, 37-38
witnesses, 48-53
  John, 54-73
  Peter in Mark, 74, 82-88
  Luke, 90
  Synoptic Gospels, 94-95